ROCK
CHALK!

KU Athletic Director Lew Perkins

"*I* have run across some magnificent young people in the 42-plus years I have been an athletic director. I would put Todd up with the highest of them. His unbelievable commitment to a sport, his unbelievable commitment to his university and to his teammates, his desire to be the very best he can in anything and everything he does. He will take on any challenge. Obviously, he loves his sport. But he loves to study. He has a thirst for knowledge. He was a finance major and an econ major. He was interested in the stock market and other things and he could talk about them. He would come in here and reel off some things, and I would think: 'Uh-oh. I have to go look at that.'

"There was just an aura about him. He was never lacking for confidence in anything he did."

*

Rising to New HEIGHTS

INSIDE THE JAYHAWKS HUDDLE

By *Todd Reesing*
with *Kent Pulliam*
Foreword
by John Hadl

Requests for permission should be addressed Ascend Books, LLC, Attn: Rights and Permissions Department, 10101 W. 87th St., Suite 200, Overland Park, KS 66212.

Photo Credits Jeff Jacobsen: Front Cover, Pages 1, 14, 23, 37, 41, 42, 107, 111, 123, 124, 125, 128, 150, 156, 157, 206 and Back Cover
Photo Credits Laura Jacobsen: Front Cover inset, Pages 8, 120, 121, 126, 127, 132, 153, 154, 158, 231
All other photos are from the Reesing Family's personal collection.
Every reasonable attempt has been made to determine the ownership of copyright. Please notify the publisher of any erroneous credits or omissions, and corrections will be made to subsequent editions/future printings.

10 9 8 7 6 5 4 3 2 1

This book is not an official publication of, nor is it endorsed by, the University of Kansas

Printed in the United States of America
ISBN-13: 978-0-9841130-6-4
ISBN-10: 0-9841130-6-1
Library of Congress Cataloging-in-Publications Data Available Upon Request

Editor: Lee Stuart
Design: Lynette Ubel

www.ascendbooks.com

Rising to New HEIGHTS

INSIDE THE JAYHAWKS HUDDLE

By Todd Reesing
with Kent Pulliam
Foreword
by John Hadl

www.ascendbooks.com

Special thanks to:

Table of Contents

He's the best we've ever had

*I*n my opinion, Todd is probably the greatest quarterback we have ever had at Kansas. He could do it all, and he did those things for three-and-a-half years. He is the most consistent performer to ever put a Jayhawk uniform on, and I've seen them all.

David Jaynes was a great passer. Nolan Cromwell was a helluva runner. But Todd could do it all. The stats verify it, and winning is the No. 1 thing, obviously.

The first time I really saw Todd was in the Colorado game when he came in when he was a freshman. I said to myself, "Who is this guy?" He came in and threw some passes, and it was obvious he was a game-breaker and made things happen. That was evident in the Colorado game.

That was sort of the trademark he had all four years he was here.

The kid just made things happen every week. He was so consistent. The things he did were so positive. He made great decisions. He had two years there where it was unbelievable the decisions he made in a split second. And he's a winner. That's what he really is.

I mean, we won the Orange Bowl one year and went to a second straight bowl game for the first time in school history while he was playing quarterback.

We've had some pretty good quarterbacks here, Frank Seuer, Jaynes, Cromwell, Bobby Douglass. I always measured our quarterbacks against Frank Seuer. Frank could run. He wasn't a great runner, but he could take off and run. He had all the passing records, and he was a tough guy.

But Todd broke all of Frank's records.

I didn't get to see a lot of games in person while I was playing in the NFL. But I saw a lot of film of David Jaynes and Cromwell. David was a drop-back passer. Cromwell was more of a runner.

You could say that Todd's skills are a good combination of those two.

Douglass, he was a big boy. He was a helluva runner. He's a tough guy. He had a cannon arm, but he would throw it 100 miles an hour to a guy 5 yards away. He doesn't have the touch.

I wasn't ever really put off by his size, 5'10" or whatever he is. I don't know what he is — maybe a little taller if he really stands straight. But he was up in Coach Mangino's office a couple of days after he had gotten into town. We shook hands. He was very enthusiastic in the way he talked and really glad to be here. You could just tell he had a thing about him that was positive and that he felt good about himself.

I had seen his high school records. You can't go by that much, but it was in one of the biggest classes in Texas. And he won big-time there.

You could see from that Colorado game his freshman year that he was a game-breaker and made things happen. I saw that right away. I was a little bit surprised the following year when Coach picked Todd to be the starter that fall. But as it progressed the next week, I could see where Coach was coming from.

The biggest thing the kid did was consistently make the right decisions with what to do with the ball, whether to run it, throw it away, or get it to another receiver. And he was always looking down the field. Even when he was scrambling he was looking for a big play. That is the sign of a really good quarterback.

And he's an exceptional kid mentally. He's a bright young man. I told him, "You want to play football, and that is great. If you make it, that is great. But in the long run with your skills and knowledge and brainpower, you could be a billionaire.

- John Hadl, former All-America quarterback at KU

This is an excerpt from an article I wrote for the Crimson & Blue *game day magazine for the Iowa State game midway through my senior year.*

(Reprinted with permission.)

*D*uring my time at the University of Kansas, I was fortunate enough to be part of some of the best years anyone could ask for during their college time. I was lucky enough to play on a team that brought the first BCS bowl victory and a 12-win season to the university, then watch as our basketball team won the National Championship that same year. I have made life-long lasting relationships with guys both on and off the football team, and I have been fortunate to work with an unbelievable coaching staff and athletic administration that starts with Lew Perkins and Coach Mark Mangino.

Of all the accomplishments my teammates and I have had over the last few years on the football field, I figured I would share some of my best memories that I am going to take away from my time at KU, both on and off the playing field.

The first thing I will always remember is all of those guys who I have spent countless hours with, working out and practicing on the field. One of the most amazing things about college football is that you have an opportunity to play with about 100 guys who make up the biggest collective family on campus.

We spend more time with each other than any of us would probably like to. But because of this, you form some of the best friendships that you ever will in your life. You find out what kind of a person someone is when they are faced with adversity and challenges in life or football, and I can tell you that most of the guys I have been fortunate to play with here at KU are not the type to shy away from a dogfight. Those are the kinds of friends you really want in life.

From my freshman year to senior year, one of the biggest transformations I will always remember is the support and excitement the football team garnered from all of the fans and alumni. To go from playing in a half-full stadium my freshman year to playing in front of sellout crowds — with even more people on The Hill watching — has been unbelievable. I have met a lot of people the last four years who tell me they would never have believed KU would have this much support and excitement surrounding the football team. Well, the truth is, we do and for that I can tell you every player and past player at KU is grateful.

As any person who has ever had a chance to play college or professional sports will probably tell you, one of the best joys in life is being able to put a smile on somebody else's face. Because I played college football, I had the opportunity to meet a lot of people in unfortunate situations and play with young kids who could care less what your record was but just like the fact you will play tag with them. That I have been able to help put a smile on a kid's face or bring some joy into the life of someone who faces challenges that far outweigh anything I have to deal with is one of the most truly rewarding things I ever got to do.

The obvious things I am sure all of you would think I might write about are hard to ever forget: beating Missouri at Arrowhead on a fourth-and-seven play that I have seen replayed many, many times in the last year — and it never seems to get old; winning the Orange Bowl on what I think is the best overall team I have ever been a part of because the game took every single person on that team to win. In this book, you will find out about more of these things in detail, and many other things I got to experience in my four years at KU.

I want to thank my parents, Steve and Debi, for the truly unwavering support you have given me my entire life, and my brother and sister, Kyle and Megan, for always being there for me as well. I thank you.

KU will forever be among the best years of my life and I want to thank my teammates, coaches and everyone who has been a part of this amazing journey the last four years.

Rock! Chalk! Jayhawk!

– Todd Reesing

Orange Bowl 1

*B*iggest game of my life, and I wake up in the morning feeling like crap. There's a lump on the side of my face so big I couldn't get a helmet over it, and I am so nauseated I don't even want to see food, let alone eat it.

How's that for a way to start your Orange Bowl game day?

But I have never missed one play in any sport from Little League to now because of injury. So it hurt, but something like that was not going to keep me out of the most important game of the season. It would have taken a lot more than that.

Ten hours later I was kneeling down on the last play of the game, and we had a 27-24 win over Virginia Tech and had proven that we were one of the best football teams in the country in 2007. It's sort of funny: in the end, we were the only one-loss team in the country with a BCS victory. Not even the national champion could say that; they had two losses that year. There wasn't anybody in the country we couldn't play with and beat on a good day that year.

We weren't even supposed to be in that game if you listened to all the experts. Virginia Tech was bigger. They were faster. They were stronger. And all that was true. They have six or seven guys from their starting 11 on defense who are playing in the NFL now.

But we were willing to put in the work, and when you are playing, you absolutely disregard what everyone is saying. We knew they were bigger, faster, stronger, but that doesn't mean anything. Everybody was saying, "They are Virginia Tech. They've got Frank Beamer. They play Beamer Ball." At the end of the day, we went out there and said, "That's bull!"

Selection Sunday

After we lost the Missouri game, we honestly had no idea where we would be going to play in a bowl. We had been hearing this and that, but that was from the media and nobody really knew anything.

The whole team was up in the donor's lounge at Allen Fieldhouse, and we were going to watch the selection show with just the team and coaches. I remember right before the show was starting, I was sitting close to Lew Perkins, our athletic director. I knew Lew a little, and I said, "How is it looking?"

He said, "You are not going to be disappointed."

That's all he said. "You are not going to be disappointed."

So I'm still in the dark, "Is it a BCS bowl ... but the Cotton Bowl is kind of amazing, too, because I am from Texas, so maybe that is it." He didn't make anything clear for me.

Right before they are about to announce it, Lew walks in holding a paper bag. We are all like, "Why does Lew have this paper bag?"

I was sitting there with James Holt and Derek Fine, who were my roommates at the time. Lew says, "I want all the seniors to stand up."

I was thinking he was going to say something like you guys had a great season and this and that ... I don't know. Then he reaches into the bag and throws an orange to Brandon McAnderson.

Everyone saw the orange fly, and then everyone just started going crazy because we obviously knew what that meant. It was kind of fun to find out right before, and it was cool the way he did it with tossing the orange.

Then they start throwing oranges to everyone. People start biting into them without peeling them. And then we hear it on the TV. It was pretty cool. There were a lot of young men jumping around like they were 3- and 4-year-olds because of how excited they were.

—◆—

Adrian Mayes, a starting guard on that team, said, "In my mind, I was for sure we were going to the Cotton Bowl. That's where I thought we were going to go. I think we were in there eating pizza, and right when they were saying it, Lew Perkins threw out some oranges to the guys. It was just awesome. We were getting the BCS game."

—◆—

Receiver Kerry Meier said he had prepared himself for anything.
"I hadn't paid attention to a whole lot of what was being said about which
bowl game we were going to go to. I was very confident and knew we had
a good athletics director who would do anything and everything possible to
get us into the best bowl game. I didn't know what to think when he walked
into the room with the paper bag. I couldn't believe it when he started
tossing oranges around. I was kind of shell-shocked."

—◆—

We knew what it meant to get to a BCS game, and we felt like we deserved it. We had one half of a single game, the first half of the Missouri game, that kept us out of the Big 12 championship. Who knows what would have happened if we hadn't had that? We knew we deserved to be there.

We continually heard people say it should have been Missouri over us and this and that. Well, they won the battle, but we won the war that season.

Boot camp

As soon as we knew we were going to the Orange Bowl, we practiced the whole month leading up to the game like we knew we were going to win. We're practicing like it's two-a-days almost. All we heard in the media was, "You guys can't win. They are bigger. They are faster. They are Virginia Tech. They got Frank Beamer. They play Beamer Ball." We were out to work harder, prepare better, and go out there and show people.

All through December we're doing conditioning, which guys hate. At that point in the season you are banged up and you want to use those few weeks to rest. But that's not the way Coach (Mark Mangino) wanted to prepare us. We had gotten to the Orange Bowl because we had put in the work, and we were going to go to the game putting in hard work.

Some teams use bowl practice to let their younger guys get some reps. We had maybe three or four practices that way with the younger guys. But after those first few practices, it was like regular season. We had three full weeks of Virginia Tech. We had the game plan in before we got to the second half of our bowl practices. We knew what we were going to do, and we were working on it for two weeks.

By the time we got to the game we knew Virginia Tech like the back of our hand, we had done it so much. Over and over. That's how Coach wanted things to be done, but I was sick of watching film of Virginia Tech and so sick of running the same plays over and over. But it all paid off because when you got into the game, it was like second nature.

Because they were so athletic, they played a really basic defense. They didn't do a lot of fancy stuff. They just lined up and said, "Come and beat us." So you knew exactly what they were going to play. We knew we were going to have to execute better than they were. We were going to have to be more prepared. We would have to have a really good game plan, and we did.

We weren't going to line up, drop back and throw the ball over their heads because we knew we wouldn't have that kind of time. And we didn't have the guys who could just run past them. But we were going to do exactly what we did all year: spread people out and run it good enough to get our nakeds and boots and mix it up.

We had a couple of days off for Christmas, which was really nice because we had been up in Lawrence through the break and had been practicing non-stop and literally doing football all day.

We had been practicing outdoors all the way through December. To this day, I am trying to figure out why we were practicing outside with snow on the field while we are getting ready for the Orange Bowl in Miami. We know there is not going to be snow down there. But that is the same hard-work mentality that Coach has. Coach wanted to practice outside. So we bundled up getting ready to play in a warm: temperature bowl.

—◆—

Mayes said, "The practices were not light. We weren't going down there to Miami or to Florida to have fun or anything. We were going down there to win this game. That was going to be the fun. But that's how Mangino prepared us for that entire year. He wasn't going to lighten up on us just because we were going to a BCS bowl game. He had been to them so many times, he knew what it took to win that game. So we were out there in the snow ... sometimes it was raining and snowing. And we're all sitting there like, 'We are not going to play in these conditions. It is going to be hot.' But we were always outside getting work."

—◆—

The first few days when we arrived in Miami, it was really hot, and the guys were having to make sure they drank fluids. Our practices were hard. We were still doing all our conditioning and wearing full pads. So you really had to take care of yourself with the fluids. But to be out there in shorts and not wear sweats and gloves was a real treat for us.

Some of our guys talked to the guys from Virginia Tech at some of the events we had, and they are out there in shorts and helmets and going through light practices. We're out there with all our pads still on. We're still running cross-fields after practice for conditioning. That kind of encompasses the whole spirit of that team. We got down to work and did it. We had been used to grinding. We were used to putting in the work. That was why we were where we were. That whole attitude of how we were practicing is what won us the game.

—◆—

Meier said, "One thing about Coach Mangino, he was never going to let us relax or be complacent. If anything, when we got down to Miami the tempo and energy level and the precision of practice and attention to detail increased even more. He hangs his hat on hard work, and we went down and definitely put some hard work in. It actually won the football game for us."

—◆—

We stayed close to Fort Lauderdale, so we didn't really get out in the night life of South Beach or anything. We had one bowling thing down there for some of the guys. But the best thing was just getting to go out on the beach and getting the sun. I think some of the guys played sand volleyball or rented Sea-Doos. But we were pretty focused on the game.

We had a curfew; the first couple of nights I think we got to stay out until 1 a.m. or so. But we had worked so hard for it, we weren't about to go out and act like fools or stay out late the week of the game because we were there to win the game.

They always say it is really fun getting into the bowl game, but it is even more fun to win one. We were not about to let all that work get away by trying to go out to South Beach or something like that. New Year's Eve, all the guys are in the hotel rooms watching fireworks out the balcony. I am pretty sure plenty of guys would have liked to go out and celebrate in Miami, but nobody did.

Meier said: "The entire week leading up to the game was great.
The way Coach Mangino handled it as far as being a business trip
and going down there to earn our respect and establish KU as a football
program was great. We went down there with our hardhats, ready to work.
I really appreciate the way Coach Mangino conducted us and our
preparation prior to the game."

—◆—

Game day

My cheek had started hurting a little bit the day before, but I just thought it might be a pimple or a bump or something. Wearing helmets all the time you regularly get bumps on your cheek. But when I woke up the morning of the game, I could feel this lump, and it's really tender.

And it's a lot bigger. I am thinking, "Man, if I had to put a helmet on right now ... "

Right after our meetings that morning I went in to see the doctor. It was an ingrown hair on my cheek that had gotten infected, like a cyst almost. The doctor tried to break it up and drain it, but it was really painful. They had to put Novacaine in the cheek just so I could tolerate the pain as they worked on it.

It was swollen up like a golf ball. I had never had anything like that before, nothing that size. The pain was just excruciating. While they are draining it, I am just sitting there gritting my teeth and grabbing on to things to hold like a little kid.

Feeling this way sucked because I had felt great all week. It was warm weather, everything was fine. Then I had this cyst and I started feeling really sick and dehydrated. They gave me a couple of IVs just to be safe, and then I went and slept for like three hours.

—◆—

Former KU tight end Derek Fine remembers that morning as well.
He felt sick, too, "Todd had been complaining about that thing on his
face, whatever. I remember looking at him and he had it and he couldn't
talk a whole lot and didn't want to move his mouth because it hurt. I just
started laughing at him. It wouldn't have been right if I hadn't laughed. In
our house, it was me and him and James Holt. If Todd ever did anything,
James and I never let him live it down."

—◆—

I woke up feeling extremely groggy at our pre-game meal. I could barely even eat anything, and I was thinking, "Oh my God. This is the absolute last thing that I want … to feel like crap before the game." I tried to eat something, but I really couldn't.

I got a Toradol injection that you often get before the game that helps you deal with pain and stuff. And once the Toradol kind of kicked in, the pain in my face and the upset feeling started to subside. And once I got to the game and out on the field, it didn't matter what I felt like because the adrenaline kicked in, and I felt great.

I felt horrible on the morning of the Orange Bowl, but gutted it out during our big win over Virginia Tech.

So I went, in a matter of about six hours, from feeling so bad to feeling so great. During the warm-ups I was probably one of the most jacked-up guys out there.

—◆—

Linebacker James Holt said there were several KU players who were sick the week of the game, "I had food poisoning three days before the game and had to sit a practice out. I didn't even get to go to some of the events on that day. I was throwing up, and they had to put some IVs in me. I definitely stayed away from the shrimp and everything after that. Todd seemed pretty normal that day, moving around and acting like himself."

—◆—

The Game

Early in the week when we got our pictures taken for the game, we were wearing our blue jerseys for the pictures. So we just assumed we would be wearing them for the game. All the players were saying wouldn't it be cool if we could wear red. Those jerseys just really look cool with those silver pants.

We didn't know we were going to wear red until we walked into the locker room and the red jerseys were hanging in our lockers, and then everybody just got really jacked up. That uniform really looks good, and at that point we hadn't lost in red yet. That added enthusiasm right before the game, which was pretty cool.

During the warm-ups there were five of my close friends from back home sitting behind our bench. My buddy Kevin (Ashmos), who probably came to more games than anybody, keeps going, "Todd! Todd! Throw me a ball!"

I look at Kevin, "I can't just throw you a ball up in the stands. I can't throw you a ball in the warm-ups."

"All right! All right! Good luck, man!"

—◆—

Ashmos, who was nearly as pumped up as Reesing, said, "He is on top of the world out there, and I could see him waving at us and stuff. I am thinking, 'He can throw me the ball. It won't be the end of the world. It wouldn't be any big deal.' So after every game after that I would always try to ask him for a ball or something to remind him of that. I think his coach even said something to him, like, 'Hey, pay attention. Quit looking over at that guy.' Me and Pat (Sanguily) were just going off."

—◆—

Everybody has some sort of nervousness before a game, but I am about as relaxed as you can be. I joke around a lot in the pre-game and stuff. I think it is the best way. You play better and you execute your plays when you are more relaxed and you are having fun. If you are out there and pressing and no one's having fun or high-fiving or celebrating, you are losing the whole point of the game.

There is this video of me in the locker room before the game, dancing around in the locker room. I was just really excited to be there, and I wanted my teammates to feel the same way. I have this motto: look good, feel good, play good.

After we went back inside, the quarterbacks and receivers are the first guys back out. I sprint out there like I always did, and I remember looking around the whole stadium and the first thing I started thinking was, "We have a whole lot more fans than they do."

That was pretty cool that we had a lot of fans who traveled a long way to be there. They showed up. They were yelling, and they were loud. That was cool because there was definitely more blue than maroon out there.

—◆—

Mayes said running onto the field was a highlight for him. "They have all these fireworks. You are coming through this tunnel, all the flashes from the cameras are going off. That is what I remember most. And afterwards the guys throwing oranges into the stands to the KU fans."

—◆—

We won the toss and took the ball and actually came out and started moving the ball. We hit B-Mac (Brandon McAnderson) on a little pass in the flat, and he turned it into a pretty good run. Derek (Fine) caught a big pass and got his helmet ripped off. I remember him getting up after the catch. Derek is a real intense guy. He just wants to line up and kick your ass.

Well, his helmet was ripped off. His eye-black was on, and he had this look on his face. He was not going to be stopped. There wasn't anybody who was going to get in his way. I remember seeing that, and it scared me a little bit. I was thinking, this guy came to play.

—◆—

"I remember that," Fine said. "I was so ticked after that. I went up and caught the ball, a really good catch and I was pumped up about it. When I was coming down and getting tackled, one of the other guys came over and ripped my helmet off as I was going down. I was fighting mad. I just started yelling and was so jacked up about it. I think it helped get the other guys fired up to see me jacked up that way. Then we all sort of relaxed and could think 'let's just go play. We are about to take this over.' I guess it worked."

—◆—

We didn't score on that opening drive, but it was a huge tempo-setter.

We knew their defense was good. We knew our game plan and what we were going to do. What we didn't know when we lined up — you never really do — is what a team is going to be like until that first snap.

We came out and got a couple of first downs and were moving the ball. All our plays were pretty much working. So even though we didn't score, having that solid first drive and not going three-and-out or getting sacked was really cool. When we came to the sideline all the guys were like, "We're feeling good."

We have a feel for their defense. We are seeing how they cover.

We had been an absolutely terrible first-drive team all year. We had scored on a first drive only once during the year. So we were never a good first-quarter team. Most games it would take a series or two to get a feel for what they were doing. But we got this from the very first drive.

— ◆ —

Mayes said the Jayhawks were a bit apprehensive.
"Not to say we were scared or anything, but listening to this and that, then you wonder whether you can play with them. Then we lined up, and we're pushing them down the field. It kind of showed us that 'Hey, we can play with these guys.' When we were able to drive the ball down the field on that series, it really set the tone for us, and guys knew we could accomplish our goals and win that game."

— ◆ —

Meier agreed. "Virginia Tech had such a stout defense that year. They were close to the top of all the categories throughout the whole year. But you kind of got that feeling from the get-go of how we moved the ball. A lot of confidence was gained on that first drive, just being able to move the ball. I think we kind of woke Virginia Tech up as well. They kind of realized 'Hey, these boys from Kansas can play a little football and they are the real deal.'"

— ◆ —

So we were playing with a lot of confidence. And then when Aqib Talib intercepted that pass and went high-stepping into the end zone, we all went nuts. At that point everybody who was playing knew we were going to win that game. We had come into the game pretty much thinking we were going to win. But as far as when that moment happened, we knew. We owned the rest of the first half.

They came out after the half with a jump in their step, had a couple of long drives when they were running the ball over and over. That's when the offense said, "Hey, the defense, we have to give them a breather. We have to do something." That's when the offense started trying to use the clock a little more.

When we got the ball at the end of the game, we knew we just had to get a couple of first downs and we had the win. That's where the conditioning comes in as a factor. You are tired. You have to dig down and say, "We have to get two first downs and we win the game."

Our offensive linemen aren't as big as the other teams, but they are more conditioned because of the running we have to do. That whole year we killed people in the fourth quarter. You could look across the field and know that the other team was more tired than we were. Knowing that, you knew you were in better condition and the fourth quarter was going to be ours. We weren't going to lose the game in the fourth quarter, and we never did. In the one game we lost, we almost came back in the fourth quarter.

So when we got the ball then, we had B-Mac and the big boys up front. We pounded them and hit a few short passes here and there. It was just a matter of executing a few more plays.

The score was only three points, but what people don't remember is that we kneeled on the ball at the 1 at the end of the game. If we had just handed the ball off we would have scored. Early in the game we got down to the 1-yard line, too, and had some bogus holding call in a big pileup. There was another play when I hit Dexton (Fields) on a long corner route. If he had just been able to get his head turned he would have gotten in. He tiptoed out of bounds at the 1. That would have been another score there, too.

It's funny because they were all pumped up with Beamer Ball and special teams, and we beat them at their own game with the fake punt and the blocked kick. We had some chances to really put it to them, but maybe it was more fitting it came down to the end.

Debi Reesing, Todd's mother, said, "That whole Orange Bowl experience was surreal, just to play on that kind of stage and that packed stadium. And, oh my gosh, what a game. It was unbelievable. You get chills thinking about the fact that you were there and you got to see it."

—◆—

Aftermath

If you know the history of Kansas football, there had been a drought when Kansas had been the doormat of the Big 12 Conference for so long. I can't tell you how many people, alumni and guys who used to play football at Kansas — people who didn't even watch football and were strictly basketball fans — who come up to me, even now, two seasons later.

Even after our not-so-picture-perfect end in my senior year, people are still saying: "You guys brought Kansas football back. We are excited to watch it again. We are excited to go to the games." It all happened because of 2007 and getting to the Orange Bowl.

The previous Orange Bowl, or a bowl of that magnitude, was 40 years before. That was seen as the last great era of Kansas football when you had John Riggins and John Zook and Bobby Douglass. It was 10 years before that when John Hadl was there.

So it had been a long time since anyone had that appreciation. Seeing how excited they were that Kansas was competitive and they had something to be excited about in the fall other than waiting for basketball season.

I've met Bob and some of those guys. But we were hearing from everyone, guys who played when it was rough in the `80s and `90s and early 2000s when they were winning two or three games. They couldn't get anybody to go to Memorial Stadium.

—◆—

Debi Reesing said, "When I think about it, I think I am most proud of the fact that he helped give some validity to KU football again in this decade. I'm not saying they didn't have some great All-America players come through their program. But that team gave some validity to the KU program and sparked the fans and alumni to return and support the team. I know what games were like his freshman year. I know he is proud of his university, and I think he is proud of his contributions to the football program. And we're proud of it, too. We're very proud of it."

—◆—

For the alumni and the guys ... for them to be excited about football for their alma mater, that is huge. They want to be proud of the school they went to and the school they played for. That is exciting to bring that excitement and get Memorial Stadium full again and be a part of the group of guys on the team that did that. That is pretty hard to top.

There are not a lot of people who can say that they helped redefine a football program.

The Border Wars

People always ask me: "Do you think the KU-Missouri game should stay at Arrowhead?"

If the environment was like that first one, then, yeah.

Sure, you always like the home-field advantage and such. But to be able to play in an environment like that, with the split stadium at Arrowhead — which is a really cool place to play — is pretty neat. And you couldn't have picked a better way to start the series if it is going to remain in Kansas City.

The Missouri game is everything a rivalry game should be. It's way different from the Kansas State game. The Missouri game is the pinnacle because of how the rivalry started, because of how close the series is, because it leads back to the Civil War.

> **"I can say the hatred and intensity of the KU-Missouri game is way higher than the UT-OU game."**

Coming from Austin, I knew the Texas-Oklahoma rivalry that they play in the Cotton Bowl every year. In having gone to the games between OU and UT at the Cotton Bowl, and having grown up going to UT games, I can say the hatred and intensity of the KU-Missouri game is way higher than the UT-OU game.

That Border War mentality is alive.

You don't realize how intense the rivalry is until you come up here and you are around it and you go to those games. And at KU, you get Coach (Don) Fambrough coming in the week of the game. For anyone who hasn't heard Coach Fambrough rant about Missouri ... he gets so fired up about the rivalry and his hatred for Missouri. You just want to strap on cleats right after he is done talking and go play the game.

Meier, who grew up along the Kansas-Missouri line in Southeast Kansas, agreed. "That first game at Arrowhead you kind of got a feel for how important and how crazy and how historical the whole rivalry is between the two schools."

— ♦ —

Megan Reesing, Todd's sister, is a freshman at the University Texas. She noticed a difference as well. "I didn't go to the OU-UT game this year, but I heard about it from all my friends. Texas-OU is definitely a hate-hate relationship. But from experiencing the KU-Mizzou games, that is a rivalry that goes deep into history. It is something that is never going to be undone. Texas-OU, you have friends who go to OU and it sometimes can be a friendly thing. But Mizzou seems like it is never going to get better. It is true hate."

— ♦ —

BORDER WAR 2007				
Missouri	7	7	14	8 – 36
Kansas	0	0	7	21 – 28

*W*hen we drove up from Lawrence for the game, people had been in the parking lot tailgating for hours. We actually got to the stadium a little later than planned because it took so long to get through the parking lot because there were so many cars and fans — even with a police escort.

As we're driving through, the Kansas and Missouri fans are all just mixed together. Our busses are coming in, and people are yelling — some cussing and some cheering for their team. We are all looking at each other asking, "Is this for real?"

This environment is going to be nuts.

— ♦ —

KU running back Jake Sharp was sitting with Reesing as the bus pulled into the Arrowhead Stadium parking lot. "You know how when you drive into Arrowhead, it is lower than the road? So we are coming down that hill into the parking lot. The sun is going down. It's getting dark out. The lights are on in the stadium, and there is not a single parking spot left in the lots. There are wall-to-wall people. The Missouri fans are flipping us off, shaking our bus. Todd and I looked at each other like, 'Man. This is it right here.'"

— ♦ —

When we got off our busses, the Missouri fans were yelling stuff at us that you don't want kids to hear. It was just crazy. And the stadium was split into black and blue. It was just the most unbelievable environment for a football game.

—◆—

Mayes said, "That atmosphere was just ridiculous. I think (ESPN) Gameday was there. It was on national TV. Earlier that day the No. 1 team lost, and I think we were No. 2. It was more than just the Border Showdown and a rivalry game. And there were Missouri fans trying to get on the bus. So many people were surrounding our bus coming in, we were late getting into the locker room to get ready for the game. I definitely felt rushed to get ready and put on my gear and get out there to warm up."

—◆—

In warm-ups it was hard to control yourself. I mean, you were so amped up and ready, you almost had to relax before the game started. Guys in the locker room are banging their heads, yelling.

We know what's at stake. We know if we win this game not only do we finish with a perfect season, after that there is a possible chance to play in the National Championship game. We had a bye week the week before the game. So everyone was rested. We had our game plan. Going in we were ready.

> **"When we got off our busses, the Missouri fans were yelling stuff at us that you don't want kids to hear. It was just crazy."**

To this day that Border War was the craziest, wildest, most intense, loud environment I have played in all four years.

—◆—

Linebacker James Holt said, "I was so amped up before the game, all the linebackers were. I am sure some people might have thought all three of us were Lawrence Taylor because we were so amped up."

—◆—

Then the game gets going, and literally everything that could have gone wrong for us in the first half did. We miss two field goals — which looking back we lost by six points. So those were huge. I had an interception where I could have had a touchdown if the ball had been thrown a couple of yards farther. I couldn't quite get enough on it. I had a tipped ball they intercepted in the first half.

The last time I threw an interception before the Missouri game was the Kansas State game. I had gone six games (213 straight passes) without an interception. It is the Big 12 record for most passes without an interception.

We get in at halftime. We have been moving the ball. We had the feeling that our defense was going to step up and get some stops. All we had to do was get going in the right direction.

We come out in the second half and start scoring at the end of the third quarter. Then we just get on a roll. We drive down the field series after series, got the game close. But they kept scoring, and we literally just ran out of time. We get that atrocious safety at the end of the game.

We get the ball at the 1 with just a few seconds left, and I get tackled in the end zone trying to make something happen. If we have two minutes, we go 99 yards and win. But we just didn't have enough time for that miracle drive like happened the next year.

Things had gone so well for so long that season. We had almost no penalties. We played disciplined ball. We played smart. We hadn't turned the ball over in weeks. In big games like that, a turnover or two, a missed field goal or two ... that makes a difference. But even if you played a bad half, it shows if you play really good in the second half like we did, you still have a chance to win.

After the game I got criticized for wearing a glove in the game. People were saying, "What's wrong with him? Why was he wearing the glove?" I don't have to make a case for why I did. I know it was the right thing. In that weather, I had a better grip on the ball. I had worn one all week in practice, and it was fine. But with the two interceptions, everyone was saying it was because of the glove. Well I also threw for 350 yards, which was my second highest total of the season, so you figure it out.

Looking back, it is such a big "What if" game.

What if we had more time?

What if we played better in the first half?

What if this and that?

What if we win the game?

That's the hardest thing looking back. That game was such a tough loss because of what could have been. But I guess it worked out in the end. The story had a proper ending with the Orange Bowl. But that game is always going to be the toughest loss.

— ◆ —

Meier agreed that it was a tough loss, but that the Jayhawks quickly shook it off to look ahead to the bowl game. "Even though that game didn't turn out the way we wanted, the one thing I really recall is that the atmosphere and feeling in the locker room after the game wasn't what an outsider might have expected. You would think that people would be down and crying, thinking the season is over. But how it was, we kind of shook that off pretty quickly. Prior to that we were 11-0. We had gone to new and great heights that KU football had never seen. Once that game was over, the mentality of the 2007 team was that we took it in and absorbed it. We took it for what it was worth. We learned from it and moved on. Sure, we would have liked to have it back and a different outcome. But we still had a heck of a great opportunity ahead of us when we got to go down to Miami and the Orange Bowl and take part in that and a BCS game."

— ◆ —

BORDER WAR 2008				
Kansas	3	16	7	14 – 40
Missouri......	0	10	13	14 – 37

*L*eading up to this game, we were coming off losing four out of five. We played Texas, Texas Tech, OU — the three teams from the South who all ended up 11-1 and all were ranked in the top five at some point in the season. We played OU really close, better than anyone had that year up until the National Championship game.

We started the season well, hit that rough skid, had that real close game with Nebraska that would have kept us in the running for the Big 12 North. But we are 6-5, and it's Missouri. Whatever happened the last five weeks didn't matter. As it goes with any KU team, if you beat Missouri it is going to be a good year.

They were already going to the Big 12 Championship game, but we still wanted to get them back for the year before. And it was still most of the same guys on their team who had played the year before.

So we are ready for it. Finishing 7-5 instead of 6-6 sounds a lot better. We were playing for a chance at a much better bowl, I guess you could say. But even if we had been 1-10, it was Missouri. We were going to get jacked up. We wanted to get them a loss and put them in a bad mood for the Big 12 Championship, where they ended up getting blown out, anyway.

—◆—

Meier said, "Coming into that game, we knew there was quite a bit at stake for us: the opportunity to get to 7-5 and become bowl eligible and it just being the Missouri week. If you couldn't get ready for Missouri, there was something wrong with you."

—◆—

Unlike the year before, we come out of the gates strong. We get an interception and a field goal on the first series. We get another score. We come out hot. They are the ones who are making the mistakes early in the game. We capitalize on their errors. It was just flip-flopped from the year before. So we go into the half with a good lead, I think it was 19-10, and knew we had more chances to score.

At the start of the second half, the weather starts picking up. It starts to snow and sleet and starts drizzling. It is really cold. We are in our all-white uniforms. Everyone is getting mud-stained and green from all the spray paint at Arrowhead to make the field look good. But they come out the second half like we did the year before.

They start clicking on offense. They are scoring and we are scoring. You flash forward to the fourth quarter, and there are four touchdowns in a row in the course of about six minutes — some of the most exciting six minutes of football you can imagine ... long drives, big plays, everything.

So we had been feeling like we had this game the whole time, the first half, halftime. Even in the third quarter we are still moving and everything is clicking. But we got stopped once and they scored. And all of a sudden you were in the middle of the fourth quarter and you think, "Holy shit! What just happened?" We had been in the lead the whole game. Now they had just crept past us.

It is back and forth. But we kind of knew on offense, the way we had been playing, it was our day. We knew if we got the ball the last time and it was going to be a shootout then we would win — at least I knew that. If we got the ball with at least a minute and a half, there was no way we weren't going to score and win.

We racked up 24 first downs against Missouri but, more importantly, we scored three more points than they did.

We had gone ahead before Missouri scored their last time. Briscoe had gotten hurt on a kickoff return, and we brought in Marcus Hereford to replace him. Marcus hasn't played much all year. We have a broken play, and I am scrambling around and hit him down the sideline where he kind of tippy-toed to stay inbounds. It was probably the biggest catch he had made in his career to that point. We're all muddy from being out there the whole game, and he had this completely white jersey and comes in and makes a huge catch. If we hadn't converted that third down and then go on and score on a pass to Kerry, the game is probably out of reach.

Now all we're hoping at this point is that our defense stops them and we run the clock out. But sure enough, they go down and score with a minute-40 or something on the clock.

So we're getting the ball back.

I remember standing over there on the sidelines with all the guys, just looking into everyone's eyes. Every person there genuinely believed we were going to score. And, of course, they were all looking at me.

— ◆ —

Meier said, "I had zero doubt we would score. This is the type of situation and moment in games that Todd thrives on. As soon as they scored, my eyes turned to Todd, and I saw that look in his eyes and saw that bounce in his step that something good was going to happen. I was so anxious to get back on the field and be out there with Todd."

— ◆ —

I am standing there, excited. It's the kind of moment you dream of as a quarterback. You want to have a chance with the ball less than two minutes, against your rival, with snow falling. You couldn't draw it up any better. I hadn't had a whole lot of chances to have that kind of comeback story in my career. The year before we killed everybody. That year we either won big or lost.

You always want that moment, to be the hero, to lead your team as the quarterback. It had been setting up this way the whole game, and then, boom, there it was under two minutes. You know you are going to throw the ball every time. It is going to be up to you and the guys blocking in front of you and the guys catching the ball.

The first play doesn't work. I scramble and find Jake. He catches it on the sidelines and gets blasted right where he had cracked ribs.

Jake is a tough kid, and you can see he was in pain. But he stayed in. I think Kerry caught the next four passes, two little short ones that they reviewed to see if he got out of bounds or was downed.

So now we have a first down deep in their territory. We're thinking we will keep driving and don't know it's the last series we would play in the game. We hit a short pass. Then I throw a long one to the end zone on second down to Briscoe on a corner route. He is right at the pylon, and two of their guys converge on him. One of them goes up and almost intercepts it. Briscoe knocked the ball away. On second down that was probably too risky a play. I am trying to make a throw that wins the game when we didn't need that yet.

So the next play is third down: "OK, let's get a first down." Briscoe came in on a little dig route. I threw it behind him. I thought he was going to sit down, and he kept moving. It wasn't even close to being caught. Now, boom, it's fourth down.

We call time out. The coaches are talking back and forth about what play to run. We don't have to go for the touchdown yet. We can get a first down, and we still have time. We are thinking they will probably go zone, so the idea is to have Kerry as the first option. The play we called we had run maybe four times all season.

—◆—

Meier said, "They had been running a certain coverage throughout the whole game. Coach dialed up the play thinking they would be in one coverage. Instead, they played a completely different coverage."

—◆—

So we get back on the field, and I see their linebackers creeping up. I'm thinking these guys are really going to blitz. Both linebackers blitz. Jake steps up to find his guy. I see Kerry, but with his guy on him man-to-man trying to spot up over the middle to get a first down isn't going to work. I look to the left, the short side of the field, and Briscoe slips on his curl route. So now, both guys are covered and I am thinking how am I going to get out of this.

There really wasn't a third option. With them blitzing, you don't have time. So I'm thinking it is in my hands. I have to make a play, scramble, whatever, or the game is over.

This actually happens a lot faster when you are doing it in the game.

So I step up. I got some amazing blocks from offensive linemen. Jake got a great block. That gave me a chance to slide back to the right. I'm looking at the rush now because I am just trying to find a way to get out of there and maybe run for a first down. I step up, and that's when my eyes go downfield.

You can tell watching the tape that their safety and the guy covering Kerry are trying to find me because they can't see me back there in the mess of things because I am too small. They take their eyes off Kerry, giving him just enough time to do what he has done all season and that is get open while I am scrambling. All he had to do was get open and get the first down. But no, he's taking off for the end zone.

—◆—

Mayes said, "The blitz they ran was something they ran in 2007 against us and got the safety. We had talked about that blitz that week, but we still didn't pick it up exactly the right way. It ended up being OK because Sharp gets a hand on the linebacker who is coming through the gap. The protection was great. I have watched the video of that play, and my explanation of his throw was like a shot put. He shot-putted the ball over the defender, and Kerry caught it."

—◆—

Meier said, "We knew we had a good match-up backside with Briscoe. But it was pretty sloppy conditions, and he couldn't make his cut clean. So I got to my depth and made my cut and turned around and saw what was going on. It didn't look all that great, bodies were just flying around. But knowing how Todd is and how he plays, I know he will be trying to make a big play. The first thing that came to my mind was put a foot in the ground and go deep. That's how Todd's mind works. He works from high to low, deep to shallow. So I put a foot in the ground and took off, and there we had it. It was kind of a bang-bang play, and to tell you the truth I don't remember how it all went down it happened so fast."

—◆—

I knew he was open as soon as I broke it. I was so worried about under-throwing it or overthrowing it that I just kind of shot-putted it up. I gingerly let go of the ball, put it up there and let him run underneath it. I was thinking, don't miss this throw, don't miss this throw. Really, you should have more confidence than that. But he was just so open, I didn't want to mess it up.

That picture, with the snow falling and the ball right up there. As soon as it went out of my hand, I knew it was over. Everyone went nuts. The celebration after the game, I went and jumped into the

This is it — the game-winning play with Kerry to beat Missouri. It's one of the most famous plays in the history of KU football.

This is the play that beat Missouri from my end.

crowd. You would have thought we just won the National Championship the guys were so excited. It made us forget about the five weeks previous to that when we lost four out of five.

I was as excited as the fans when we beat Missouri at Arrowhead.

———◆———

Megan Reesing said, "That game-winning touchdown was the most excited I have ever been at a football game. My brother (Kyle) and I were just jumping and holding on to each other and screaming. We were at the opposite end of the field and couldn't really see what happened. We had to watch it on the Jumbotron. But we were all just going nuts over there.

"When you watch a game that is close and there is a minute left, every possible scenario runs through your head. You always hope for the best. I knew that when Todd started marching them down the field and they were in the red zone they had that chance. I knew Todd would find a way to make a receiver get open and make something happen."

———◆———

Just to beat Missouri and know they are feeling down in the dumps like we did the year before is great. It puts you in a great mood for the month before the bowl game. That was definitely the most exciting game I played in the whole time because of getting a chance to make that last-minute drive and having a play that really defines the season, a play that will be re-played for years and years. People will tell you that was the most exciting game they ever watched of KU football. To be a part of that and be a guy who made the last play. That whole drive was just such a special moment to be a part of. After Missouri scored, we were on the sideline, and I remember high-fiving every one of the offensive linemen, talking to the receivers. I am almost laughing at them, smiling and grinning. To me, that was exciting. I am thinking, this is what you play for. This is why you sign up to play football so you can be in the moment like this.

I just remember nodding my head. I said, "You guys already know we are going to score. We just have to go do it. It's already happened. We just have to go execute." Everyone is getting focused, thinking, "I am going to do my job. That's what I have to do." I could tell by looking at those guys there was no way we were not going to score.

— ◆ —

Sharp said, "We were just beat to pieces that year.
I don't think Todd or I practiced the week before the game.
I had like two cracked ribs, and Todd couldn't throw all week.
But it got to the game, and it's like,
'All right man. Let's give it a shot.' When they scored at
the last, we were like, 'Phew, we're in two-minute, baby.
The pressure is on. This is clutch time.' Well, that is where
Todd thrives. It's where Kerry thrives. So we weren't even really
concerned about it. We can score, there is not an issue. We got this,
and we did chop, chop, chop, chop. That last play, there
was definitely some God-given luck. But that was just Kerry
and Todd knowing exactly what the other was going to do.
They could tell what the other guy was thinking pretty much."

— ◆ —

You can tell when someone looks back at you whether they believe or not. I could tell those guys, all the offensive linemen, the receivers, knew I was telling the truth. They believed it, too. They believed if we have this guy out there making plays behind center, we like our chances. It was like an unspoken thing that everyone knew we were going to score. They all believed it. You could see it in their eyes. It was just a matter of doing it.

— ◆ —

Mayes said, "I was actually right by Todd when Missouri scored. You know, a lot of times the offensive line stood close to Todd just to be ready. Todd looked at us and said, 'We have enough time to score, and we are going to do it.' I could see on the sideline, there were some of the other offensive players who were down a little bit, and the defensive players coming off the field, you could see they were upset. But the six guys who were standing there, Todd and the offensive linemen, we were ready. Todd was like, 'We are going to do this and we are going to do it right now.'"

— ◆ —

Gun treo right, lucky menu 3

This play beat Missouri in the 2008 Border War, when Reesing completed a touchdown pass to Kerry Meier on fourth-and-seven in the fourth quarter.

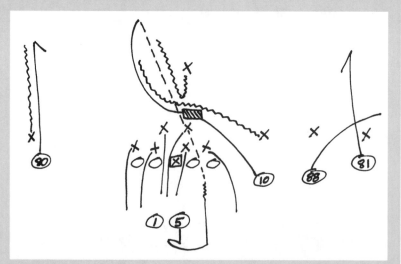

*W*e had called a timeout, and our idea was that we would try to get a first down. Kerry Meier (10) was running a spot route over the ball where he can work the zone. Dezmon Briscoe (80) is on a curl, and we have another curl route and a flat route at the right.

Jake (1) has a swing route, unless his guy blitzes.

Kerry is really good at working the zones and finding a way to get open. If he's not, it's an easy transition to get to Briscoe. We rode Kerry and Briscoe the whole game. If they can't get open, then, Todd, you'd better find something to do. We were thinking they would go zone and make us try to squeeze the ball into a tight window.

Instead, they blitz both the linebackers on what's called a double dog. The safety rolls to the middle of the field, and they are playing "Cover One" or "Man Free," which means every receiver or running back is covered by a man and there is a safety behind. It becomes four guys covering four guys with one guy spying the middle of the field.

As I drop back, I see they are blitzing. The man covering Kerry is squeezing him tight, and you won't be able to jam the ball in there. The safety is creeping up because he is watching the 7-yard mark and ready to jump a route right at the (first down) sticks.

So I take my eyes over to Briscoe because he's man-to-man on a curl route, and Briscoe is going to win that battle. All he has to do is push 12 yards up the field, come back and use his big frame to shield the ball and make the catch for the first down.

As my arm is going forward, he slips at the top of his break. At the same time, I see these linebackers starting to cross my face and now we are back to ground zero with the play having gone completely to crap.

All but one of the rushers were being pushed to the left, so I come back to the right and this lane opens up. I was able to step back up where it was opening. I guess their safety thinks I am going to take off running, so he steps up. The guy covering Kerry loses him, maybe because he sneaked a look at me, too.

Kerry sees me scrambling and knows he has to get open. I know he is open, and it is a matter of lobbing it ever so gently over the top. All our guys picked up the blitz, doing a fantastic job.

Once I saw Briscoe slip, the only thing in my mind was get out of the pocket, improvise and just make a play — basically do what I love doing, which is backyard football. That's where having someone like Kerry, who had been a quarterback, is really helpful. He knows he has to get open, and he knows I am probably coming to him because that's what I did all season. Whenever I was scrambling, I guarantee more than half of them went to him.

BORDER WAR 2009				
Missouri	3	10	20	8 – 41
Kansas	14	7	7	11 – 39

*W*e come into the game having lost six in a row, and yet again that means nothing. This is Missouri. We have to win to go to a bowl game. We have been on a pretty rough skid, and none of the seniors want to go out this way.

We want to go out with a win. We want to go to a bowl game, even if it is as a 6-6 team. We want a chance to finish the season with two wins and go out with our third consecutive bowl, which would be another milestone we could accomplish.

We couldn't have started any better. Whatever we did on offense worked. We were scoring left and right, throwing the ball all over the place. I think we passed the first 11 plays in the game. We were just going to sling the ball around, and it was working.

I was in the zone as a quarterback. I knew what the defenders were going to do before they knew. I was hitting all the passes, plays were working, guys were getting open and we felt we were in control most of the game again.

We get into the second half. Briscoe had a couple of fumbles — one at our 5-yard line and they get an easy score off that. We have another one when we are driving. Yet again, a few plays, a few turnovers, only this time it was in the second half. We couldn't get a couple of stops on defense and they climb back into the game.

We're trailing 36-28 in the fourth quarter when I hit Briscoe on a 73-yard touchdown pass and then tie the game with a two-point conversion. We go ahead when Jake Branstetter hits a field goal.

They punt, and with about three minutes left in the game we get the ball back at our 1 with a three-point lead. People have all asked about the play calling on the last three plays. We had been moving the ball, and I think what they were thinking is that Coach Warinner was going to put the ball in my hands.

So the first play, we actually have a chance at hitting Briscoe. The throw wasn't there, the route wasn't quite there. So we come back on second down.

Most people would say OK, you tried your shot, go ahead and run it. Well, we come right back at Briscoe, who already had 240 yards receiving that day. Just run a hitch route. He catches it, at least gets 6-7 yards, better than any run play we could have had. If the guy misses the tackle — and they missed a bunch that day — who knows. You get a first down and you are back in business.

What are the odds? He falls to his knees and the ball goes right over his hands. It's the most routine route. You go five yards, stop and catch the ball. Because of whatever reason, he slips and it doesn't work.

Then we come back on third down and call a quarterback draw. The thinking here was that they are probably going to go soft and not let us get a first down, make us punt and give themselves a chance. We had done one earlier in the game and it had been probably our best running play the last four or five weeks. I had run one earlier in the game for like 16 yards.

So I drop back in the end zone. Their two defensive tackles just got a huge push. They just collapsed the pocket, and they did it so fast. I saw it collapsing, and I took off fast. I still think I got out of the end zone ... that's debatable. If our guards hold a little longer, who knows. Maybe we get a first down. But for sure you aren't going to get a safety.

So then we have to kick it. Now we have a one-point lead, and our defense has to get a stop. They don't, and Missouri's kicker hits a 27-yard field goal with no time remaining to win by two.

*Meier said he also had no qualms with the play calling, even
though the series used little time off the clock. "Those three plays were
plays we had run throughout the entire game, and they had worked the
whole game. I can't fault Coach Ed Warinner going after those plays
because of the success we had with those plays. Of course, you would like
to have them back at this point. But the success we had with them prior to
the last series I am definitely with Coach Warinner in making those calls.
Who knows what would have happened if we had run the ball ...
there are a lot of what-ifs if we had done something else."*

———◆———

The game ended up the way the whole season kind of ended up,
you know. Things didn't go our way the whole season. So, in a way,
it was almost fitting that we blow it in the Missouri game with a few
plays.

It was just terrible. We genuinely thought we were going to win
it, get to a bowl game, beat the crap out of someone at a bowl game
because we were much better than a 6-6 team. If we could have done
that, finish 7-6, win three straight bowls, have three winning seasons,
everyone is going to forget about that year.

They would talk about our senior class, **"To have everyone
go out fighting, at
least we showed our
true character."**
our third straight bowl, all the stuff we accomplished. Instead, it took our senior class
— which did accomplish more than any
other team with the Orange Bowl and the
Insight Bowl and a share of the Big 12 North — and turned it into
how many games we lost the last year. They didn't get to a bowl game.
The coach ended up resigning.

It was several months before people even started saying, "Let's
look at what they accomplished and not how they ended their last six
games." What sucked is that no one wanted it to end that way.

It is kind of fitting that the last Missouri game I would go and
throw for almost 500 yards. I had five touchdowns and ran for another. I would have loved to have gone on to a bowl game. But at least
you go out fighting and have your best day and throw for more yards
than anyone has thrown for. Kerry got a mild concussion and still
got back in the game. To have everyone go out fighting, at least we
showed our true character.

The
Early
Years

3

CHAPTER

*F*ootball is my sport now, but when I was growing up my parents made sure I was exposed to almost every sport you can think of. My brother, Kyle, and I were extremely active, and I played soccer, tennis, swam, did gymnastics when I was real little, played golf, baseball, football. I used to rollerblade and skateboard and played roller hockey in the street.

Todd vaulting over the horse during an early attempt at being a gymnast.

If it was outdoors, and in Austin everything was outdoors, it was something I was going to do. Growing up, I had more golf trophies than any other sport. Then I became more interested in basketball, then baseball and, finally, football.

But unlike a lot of Texas football players, I didn't start playing tackle until I got into junior high school. I never played on any of the Pop Warner teams. We were playing flag football.

— ◆ —

Steve Reesing, Todd's father, said, "I had them play every sport they could play to see what they would be interested in. I played golf, so I had them playing golf with me when they were young. They were both really good at it as real young kids. But we were just trying to introduce them to things to see what drew their fancy in the end.

Todd and his father/coach Steve Reesing on an all-star baseball team.

*"I grew up playing predominantly baseball and football. In the end,
Todd gravitated towards football and Kyle went towards baseball —
though they both played both sports through high school.*

—◆—

I was a big kid

You wouldn't know it by looking at me now, but I was a really big kid. I was one of the bigger kids in elementary school. If that were still true today, I might be a few million dollars richer.

But no kidding, when the doctor gives you his little charts, I was like in the 80th percentile or something — which apparently doesn't mean anything since I didn't turn out that much bigger. But I was the kid in 4th grade who started sprouting armpit hairs before anyone else.

Todd in an elementary school photo.

My brother is two years older than I am, and I think that's where I really got my competitive streak because I was always trying to beat him. I'd go and tough it out with the older, bigger boys and play sports with them. And of course with my brother, no matter what we were doing, we had to beat each other.

—◆—

*Kyle Reesing said, "Even with him being bigger for his age, with
the two years I was older really makes a big difference. We were both very
competitive, and I never held anything back in that regard.
That is where he really got the attitude of 'I'll prove you wrong' from
an early age because he was always trying to compete with me and my
friends in anything and everything."*

—◆—

We had a big yard in a downtown area of Austin called Tarrytown, and football started by playing catch in the yard with my Dad and my brother. Golf was what I was really focused on when I was younger, before you start playing on all the select baseball teams in the summer. Me and my friends would go up to Lions Municipal, this local course a few minutes from my house, and we would play golf five or six days a week. You'd get $20 from your mom, then go up and play 18 or 36 holes every day. They had a summer-long cheap fee. We'd get a hamburger at the turn and play golf all day.

I had more golf trophies as I was growing up than any other sport. There was some kind of tournament there every week, and I finished high in tons of tournaments. I won the city championship for my age a couple of times when I was 8 to 11 years old or so. One year, my partner and I won it in doubles. I had tons of golf trophies from all the city championships. I have a few buddies who stuck with golf, and a couple of them have ended up playing in college. Back in the day I was beating up on them, but if I went and played with them now I think they would beat me by about 15 strokes.

Todd (right) and Kyle showing off their city golf championship trophies.

I played on a couple of AAU basketball teams that were pretty dang good. The first team I played on we were kind of an all-white suburban team of kids. We were really good. Back then, we had some guys who were a lot bigger than anyone else. That was back in the day when I could play basketball pretty decently.

There was a period of time when basketball was my love. It was kind of weird. I changed from sport to sport which one I liked the most. One time it was golf. One time it was basketball. One time it was baseball. It ended up being football as the last one I loved.

—◆—

Boyhood friend Andrew Williamson said, "He was a freak at everything from a really young age. He was the guy who ... baseball, football, basketball, he was just a freak from second grade on. I am a big golfer, and he used to beat me in the city golf tournaments. I mean, I am playing golf all year, and then he comes out and whips us. He's not the biggest guy or the strongest guy, but he has this 'X factor' and it has been going on since he was pretty young."

—◆—

Another friend, Pat Sanguily, agrees. "He was just so electric when he gets involved in a team or involved in anything. He was still getting letters for baseball after he didn't play for an entire year. I have seen the golf trophies, which sucks because golf is my sport. But I would go play him, and he hasn't picked up a club in a year or so, and he would just turn it on. I am like, 'How did you do that?'"

—◆—

The football games really started when I was in third grade. My brother and all his friends were in the fifth grade. We would go up to the elementary school, which was not too far away, and we would play full contact tackle football, just the kids. Even then I didn't shy away from anything. I would bring it on myself. I wanted to get my hands on the ball and try to make someone tackle me. I wasn't afraid to run at someone full speed ahead.

Kyle Reesing said that experience helped tremendously.
"At an early age, if you can go out and compete with kids who are two years older than you and have success, it definitely helps your confidence. You think, 'Hey, I can play with these guys.' Just because they are two years older, you don't need to be intimidated by them. Just go out and show you can play, and they will respect you for it."

—◆—

Steve Reesing remembers that both boys were top athletes.
"They were typical brothers, two years apart. The other thing that helped both Todd and Kyle was that they were not only able to compete, but they were able to make teams at a higher level at an early age. I think it helps you in your athletic career if you have an opportunity to play against more mature kids because it brings you along faster. We always assumed Todd was going to be significantly bigger when he finally matured because he always graded out in the 90th percentile, and we were thinking maybe he may have taken more from Debi's side of the family which was bigger than my side of the family. In the end both Kyle and Todd ended up being pretty much the same size."Fortunately, they were both equally athletic. So in any game they could play, there was going to be competition."

—◆—

Organized football

Being on the playground or out in the yard was really the earliest football days because I didn't play in any of the Pop Warner leagues or anything like that when I was growing up. A lot of my friends did, but me and my brother never did. It was all just in the yard or up at the elementary school. The first actual organized football I did would have been flag football at WAYA (West Austin Youth Association).

—◆—

Steve Reesing said the parents in Tarrytown opted for the flag-football leagues. "We had some pretty athletic kids in the neighborhood we competed in. James Street, the UT quarterback, had twin boys who were the same age as Kyle. Another UT quarterback, Randy McEachern, had a son who was a good friend of Kyle's and played on our team. So even though you would think you'd be playing Pop Warner football in Texas, most of the dads elected to go with flag football instead of tackle football."

—◆—

I went to a private school called St. Stephens in 6th grade, which also had flag football. Another kid from the same neighbor-

hood (Scott Roudebush, who played college golf at TCU) beat me out for the quarterback spot. So my first year playing for a school or a team, I wasn't even the quarterback. I got beat out, and was out there "Randy Moss-ing" it.

I remember catching a pass against our big rival, last-second play of the game. He threw up a big bomb to me, and I caught it up over the top of somebody and pulled it down in the end zone to win the game. All of us 6th-graders were out there going crazy.

Todd (left) and his brother, Kyle, skiing on a trip to Austria.

— ◆ —

Pat Sanguily, one of his longest friends, remembers playing athletics against Todd before actually knowing who he was. "I didn't actually meet him until we were in 7th grade. I had gone to St. Gabriel's for middle school. I remember him from sixth grade, thinking, 'Who is that athlete out there?' I think he was playing wide receiver. Another guy (Roudebush), who plays golf at TCU now, was playing quarterback for them."

— ◆ —

We moved to Lake Travis before I was entering the 7th grade. So the first time I actually played tackle football, I was in the 7th grade. I came out and won the quarterback job there in 7th and 8th grades.

We had a pretty good team. We had a really good receiver, a guy named Fred Robinson, who ended up being the guy I threw to from 7th grade on. He was undersized like me, real small (5'8", 160), real fast, real quick, great hands. He ended up leading the state in yards, catches and touchdowns. My connection with him kind of started there. There was only one other middle school in our district, so the guys I started playing with in 7th grade continued on through high school. We all kind of started the bond there in 7th grade. I was the quarterback. I was the kicker. I was the punter and in middle school you have to play both ways, so I was the middle linebacker.

Todd's 8th grade football photograph.

The first game I ever played was against our rival, which was Dripping Springs Middle School. They scored a late touchdown to go ahead 12-7 — because in 7th grade no one could make extra points. After their touchdown, I get the kickoff return and almost run it back. The kicker tackles me. We hit a couple of passes, and then we call our favorite play — which I can still remember to this day. It was called 10-80-FSO. I don't know how I remember that.

No one was open. We're on about the 12-yard line. Time is expiring. I take off running, and I jump up on top of this guy right at the goal line and fall down on him in the end zone. We win the first game we played over our rival. I throw my helmet off there and pretend like I was an NFL superstar. It was my first tackle football game, so I sort of started my tackle football career — not on a heroic note, but at least on a last-minute finale basis.

— ♦ —

Steve Reesing said, "I had played quarterback in high school, but I was not nearly the caliber either of them were. So they both gravitated toward quarterback during their youth leagues. That was probably a function of me always going out and playing catch with them. We were either playing catch with the baseball or with the football. We had a game we used to play called body parts. As we were throwing the ball we would get farther and farther apart. You would get one point for hitting the body torso and two points for hitting the head. The first one to 10 wins. The idea was that throwing the ball, you had to be accurate."

— ♦ —

High School

When I go to high school, football isn't a very big thing at the school. Our school had never won a district championship in its 20-something years. We were a 4A school. We border the district where West Lake High School is — where Drew Brees went to high school. West Lake was the one that always dominated in Austin and did things in the state. Our schools never played, though they started playing a few years ago when our school started getting really good. Now Lake Travis has kind of taken over as the power there.

My freshman year, our school went 0-10; didn't win one game. My brother was a junior, and he played quarterback. There was no one in the stands. No one went to the games. It was pathetic. People made fun of football players — exactly like they did at Kansas. Most of the guys who played didn't even care. They just played because they liked football.

The next year they brought in Jeff Dicus, who was my coach. He had a knack for building football teams. He had been to three different programs that had all been terrible like our school was. And he had found a way to turn them all around. He came into a situation sort of similar to what Coach Mangino did at Kansas.

Todd Reesing with his brother, Kyle (left), with their Troy Aikman-signed footballs.

The first thing Coach Dicus did was establish discipline. He kicked guys off the team who weren't doing things the way he wanted and the right way. He kicked off guys who weren't willing to work hard or play as a team. He brought in a whole new coaching staff, a whole new philosophy. And a bunch of guys in my brother's class ended up getting booted off the team because they weren't doing things the right way — guys who were probably some of the better athletes. But he made an example and said, "We are not going to have that."

He had to establish discipline. He knew if he let guys just keep doing whatever they wanted, it would never get better. If he let the cool guys get away with stuff, then no one else would do it right, either. So he put in the discipline. He was hard-nosed and he wasn't afraid to cuss guys out or punish them.

The offensive coordinator came with him, and his son was a quarterback. So my brother, who had been the quarterback when he was a junior, switched and ended up playing defensive back. He ended up leading our team, had like 120-some tackles that year. But he was really more worried about baseball at that point. He was playing football for fun.

I am the backup quarterback. But I have never known what sitting on the bench feels like, and I can't do that. I say, "Coach, could I play receiver?" I had done it before. I just wanted to get on the field. I end up winning a receiver's spot and end up going on to being all-district as a receiver — had like 46 catches for 750 yards and six or seven touchdowns. I am actually the leading or second-leading receiver on the team.

That year we go 3-7, so we make progress in the season. The first game I play in varsity, I am the kicker. We are playing our first game against a 5A school that was supposed to beat us pretty good. My buddy Kevin is going to that school. But we score a touchdown late in the game to tie it up, and all I have to do is make the extra point to win the game.

I push-spray it right of the upright about a foot or two. I am thinking, these older guys are going to kill me for blowing the game in our first game under a new coach. Sure enough, we go to overtime and lose. So I blow the first varsity game I ever played in high school. It was just terrible.

—◆—

*Kyle Reesing said, "Yeah, I remember that. But you're not ticked off —
and if anybody had tried to say something to him, I would have hit them in
the face. Not one person loses the game. There were opportunities for our
offense to score another touchdown or our defense to get another stop."*

—◆—

*Lake Travis football coach Jeff Dicus said,
"He handled it really well, you know, the way a head coach would
want you to if you had to draw up a model of how a kid should react
to some adversity. Todd handled it very well."*

—◆—

As the season goes on, we are competitive in games, but we just never can find a way to win them — quite similar to my senior year at KU.

The guys are playing hard, but we have a lot of younger guys on the varsity that year because of all the guys the new coach had kicked off. So we know we have the makings of potentially a really good team.

Player of the year

So we come back the next year. I make the transition back to quarterback. Playing receiver actually helps that next year going back to quarterback because you have a feeling for what those guys are doing out there. You know exactly how much the timing of the routes mean, what the receivers are looking at and then you can put it all together as a quarterback. Those two positions have to be more coordinated than anybody for what they are trying to accomplish.

—◆—

"He was a great quarterback as a freshman, but my offensive coordinator was coming with me, and his boy was the quarterback," Dicus said. "We talked to Todd about moving to the receiver position to help him learn the offense. It would be the best maneuver for us and for him and his future as a quarterback. Because of his year at receiver, it really elevated his level as a quarterback because he understood the offense from a receiver's standpoint. He understood coverages better. It helped him to perform really well."

—◆—

My first game as a starting quarterback, I throw two interceptions and we lose the game to a team we should have beaten. It's a really rough start for me. I am down on myself. My coach, who was a great coach and mentor, stayed on me. He was so particular about details and how you read defenses, and he was an incredible teacher. We are breaking down film, doing fundamentals, hitting the weight room at 7 in the morning — all the stuff you need to do to have success.

Dicus said, "He was trying to do too much himself, and he wasn't trusting the system and wasn't trusting his teammates. I think, from that game forward, if memory serves me right, he had like two or three interceptions the entire year. He really grew leaps and bounds from that game. He understood there are 10 other guys around him who will enable him to have more success. I think that was kind of an eye-opener for him. He was one of those guys who came in early for films. We really studied. He has a great memory, and as a result of him being coached up through the week as far as tendencies the defense was going to give us, he knew when to switch out of plays and change things at the line of scrimmage and we were really able to do a lot of good things."

—◆—

When I got to KU, I'd be talking to guys who went to Kansas schools. They hadn't heard of any of this. They didn't even watch films on their opponents. But I was in before practice with the coach, who was also the quarterbacks coach, breaking down film. After that first game, I kind of settle in. We only lose one game the rest of the season, go 8-2 and win the district title for the first time ever at our school.

—◆—

Kyle Reesing said, "Coach Dicus really took Todd under his wing and trusted him to be the player he knew he could be. Todd worked for it, too. It definitely helped contribute to a lot of success and really helped build up his confidence to show a lot of people he could play."

—◆—

Steve Reesing said, "The previous coach we had was not a passing-oriented coach. With Dicus coming on board, he brought in a true spread passing offense to this high school."

—◆—

We get to the playoffs and lose a heartbreaker to a high school from San Antonio. That team has a bunch of guys I was friends with, so I am playing against guys who are my friends. We play in the Alamo Dome, which is really cool. It was the first time any of us has done something like that.

We lose, and we are upset about that. But our senior class that really kind of got things turned around, is coming back for the next year.

So I think the season is over, and I'm looking ahead. That was the year that I won 4A Player of the Year in the state of Texas. I had no idea I was even up for consideration for something like that. I knew I had good numbers. But we just came out of no-where. No one knew any-thing about Lake Travis.

A couple of girls who were friends from school came over to the house, and we were meeting up to go out and eat or something. One girl came into the house and said: "Oh, congrats on the 4A player thing."

Todd's junior year photo at Lake Travis High School.

I said: "What are you talking about?"

She said: "My mom was watching TV, and you won like some player of the year thing."

That was the first I had heard of it. I guess her mom had seen it on the news and told her. I was standing next to my Dad and asked if he knew what she was talking about. We went in and looked it up on the news, and sure enough, I was 4A State Player of the Year. What's funny is that same year Chase Daniel was the 5A Player of the Year.

"When he moved into the quarterback spot, nobody really knew anything about him as far as any college recruiters because he hadn't played," Steve Reesing said. "The first idea I had that Todd was good enough to be a college player was as we went through that junior season."

—◆—

Senior year

So we get to my senior year. We have a lot of people back, and expectations are really high. After winning that first championship in our junior year and then losing in the first round of the playoffs, we're thinking it's going to get much better this year.

In our first scrimmage, we lose Luke Lagera, our running back who had rushed for over 1,000 yards. He was very similar to Jake Sharp, really fast and elusive. He tears his ACL in the first scrimmage. So that is a big blow to the team, and the pressure kind of falls on me and Fred Robinson, the receiver I have been throwing to since seventh grade.

—◆—

"It really made him have to step up his game to another level," Dicus said. "There was more responsibility thrown on him because we lost our stud tailback. But he had some good kids around him receiver-wise. He did a great job of handling that."

—◆—

High school friends Andrew Williamson, Pat Sanguily and Logan Henderson help Todd celebrate his 18th birthday at Cool River, a restaurant in Austin.

We're running the spread, we are shotgun every snap. We have either four or five receivers. When Luke goes down, so does our running game. So the running game falls on me. I become the leading rusher and the quarterback.

Back then, I was bigger. I weighed more in my senior year in high school than I did when I was a junior or senior in college. So I am just bulldozing people. There is one play when I stiff-arm a kid, and I literally got my hand on one side of his helmet and throw him to the ground. I end up rushing for close to 1,000 yards my senior year.

We are killing everybody in our non-conference. In the 12 games we play, I think I only play into the fourth quarter three or four times. A lot of times I only play for a series or two in the third quarter before my coach takes me out because he was not a big proponent of running the score up. So we are killing everybody. We are ranked in the state. In the first five games I have 20 touchdown passes and zero interceptions.

The games are like practice. We are joking around — really pretty much like the KU game against Nebraska in 2007. But it is every game. We can score at will, and people can't play with us.

We got into district, have a couple of close games, but we finished the season undefeated. It's funny, freshman year we are 0-10, senior year 10-0. It is a complete turnaround in three years.

Instead of having no one at the games, we're selling out everywhere we play. People are going crazy for football. We have more fans at away games than some of the home teams. A football frenzy just takes over in Lake Travis. People who didn't even have kids would come to the games. It blew up, literally happened over night. It became the place where people went to socialize before they went to parties later on. People were cheering, and face-painting and making shirts and all sorts of stuff.

It was an exciting year. But what's funny is that after the season ends, my stats are staggeringly better than my junior year when I was 4A Player of the Year. My senior year I threw for 3,400 yards, 41 touchdowns and like 5 interceptions. I led the state with a 72.6 completion percentage. I wasn't even honorable mention All State. The 4A player of the year that year was Matthew Stafford (Highland

Park HS/University of Georgia/Detroit Lions). I think the second place guy was Jevan Snead (Stephenville HS/Texas/Mississippi/Tampa Bay Bucs) who ended up at Ole Miss.

You go from being the 4A Player of the Year, your team goes undefeated, you have way better stats and you don't even get honorable mention. I was the Central Texas Player of the Year for all classes. But statewide, I didn't even get a nod. I was third-team all-state punter.

—◆—

"We had a hard time trying to understand the logic behind him not receiving more honors than what he did," Dicus said. "But you know, that's kind of the sports writers' world. Sometimes it goes your way and sometimes it doesn't. That was something that was kind of unexplainable to all of us."

—◆—

Was it politics? Duh. Both of them were 6'3" or 6'4". I think they had Stafford as the No. 1 overall high school recruit in the nation. Snead was one of the top-ranked quarterbacks. My stats were better or as good as theirs. At that point, I had already committed to Kansas. But that was pretty disappointing for me.

—◆—

Kyle said, "If you are going to lose out to somebody, why not it be to the No. 1 overall pick in the NFL draft and the starting quarterback for an NFL team? But, yeah, that was pretty disappointing for all of us."

—◆—

Topping a hard act to follow

The similarities between Todd Reesing and his brother, Kyle, extended beyond the athletic field. Both graduated No. 4 in their high school class — the result of Debi Reesing's emphasis on academics. Their younger sister, Megan, was a freshman when Todd was a senior at Lake Travis.
She goes them one better by the end of her senior year.
She said, "Coming into high school I was already known as 'Little Reesing' because of my older brothers. Because Todd graduated in December his senior year, I thought OK, Todd is gone and now I can be just the 'new' Reesing. But for continuity's sake they just called him Todd and me Little Reesing.
"Having Todd, both my brothers really, be so successful in athletics really pushed me to succeed on my own. I wanted to be like them.

I wanted to have that success and those accomplishments.
I ended up doing well and graduated near the top of my class.
I really forced myself to do well academically.
"Then my senior year, I ended up getting all-state in volleyball.
My volleyball team made the state tournament, reached the semifinals.
So I definitely beat them on that mark and I get to shove that in their face.
I was the only Reesing kid to make it to the state semifinals in their sport."

—◆—

Away from the field

Reesing has five really close friends who all grew up in Austin:
Kevin Ashmos, Patrick Sanguily, Andrew Williamson, Logan Henderson,
and R.W. McDonald. Strangely, none of them attended
Lake Travis High School. They remain close.

—◆—

The friendship started when we were so young, and I have always gotten along with those guys so well that the fact we didn't go to the same high schools didn't really matter. We always met up on weekends, whether they came out to my school or I went in to where their school was. It didn't matter. We all have common interests, never really fought or argued about anything. So it makes sense that we would still be friends all the way through college even though none of us goes to the same college. When we meet up back in Austin over the holidays or the breaks, we see each other and it's like we had known exactly what the other person was doing all the time.

I have known Kevin since I was about 6 because we played little league baseball together on the all-star teams ever since our first year. I don't know if we were ever on the same team. But our dads always coached, and you knew everybody who was on those teams.

Andrew, we went to elementary school together and met in the third or fourth grade. We lived only a few blocks from each other and we would ride our bikes down to Pecos Street in the Tarrytown area of Austin and meet at the same corner to go riding or roller-blading or whatever we were doing. We were real active back in the day. So I met both those guys really young and have always been good friends with them.

I actually met Patrick through Andrew. We all became really good friends. We all four started out at different high schools, though. Then after two years, Pat transferred and went to the same high school as Andrew. But we stayed good friends the whole time.

—◆—

Kevin says, "When I tell people that Todd didn't go to my high school, and Andrew and Pat didn't go to my high school, they are kind of weirded out by it because it wasn't the way they did it with their longtime friends."

—◆—

Patrick said, "It's kind of weird how the dynamic of our group of friends from back home got together. A lot of us met through sports. Todd and I had another friend in common, and Andrew introduced Todd and I. We all just kind of became best friends immediately. Everybody brought something to the table. My buddies at college are always surprised how close we are with our friends back home. But we have a great time together. Todd and Andrew and I went to visit a friend of ours at the University of Georgia. We all went to dinner and literally laughed for two hours. We weren't even drinking or anything. We just enjoyed each other's company so much."

—◆—

Andrew said, "At one point or another, all of us had gone to the same school. But then we all left and went to other schools. He moved up to Lake Travis. I went to O'Henry, Kevin and Patrick went to Austin High. It was funny how it all came together because most people are good friends with people they went to high school or college with. My best friends, you named them, and it is going to be like that for life. It is something unique we have."

—◆—

During the season me and Kevin talked at least twice a week. He was a huge football fan, so I was talking to him about what was going on. The other guys, we would talk every couple of weeks to see what is going on or what's new or if someone had a funny story or just wanted to make plans over the holidays. The first three guys were my first friends. But Logan and R.W. were just as much a part of the big group. Logan went to the same high school as Kevin. R.W. went to a different high school from all of us.

I didn't have any classes in the spring after my senior year, and we all went to Georgia to see Logan. We sat and laughed for two hours.

—◆—

Kevin said, "We're all different, and we're all the same in some way. My life is more centered around sports than probably Todd's is. He plays football and stuff, but all I care about is sports and the social aspect of stuff. Pat kind of puts together the best of both worlds with studies and his social life. And Andrew is kind of similar to Pat in a lot of ways."

—◆—

Andrew said, "Our group of friends kind of concentrated around Austin High because those are the girls we hung out with. But we did stuff out at Lake Travis, too. Those were really the two hot spots. But Todd spent more time coming into Austin from Lake Travis than we did going the other way."

—◆—

All agree that there was no way to foresee Reesing's success at Kansas. Ashmos said, "There was no way I could have told you he would have won a BCS game and all that stuff. I did know that if he got a shot, he would succeed. He found the right situation, and he got a chance. I was ticked at Texas and SMU for not recruiting him. Teams like TCU passed on him, and that kind of irritated me. When he told me he was going to Kansas, I didn't know anything about the football program there except that Texas beat them up every year."

—◆—

Sanguily echoed the thought. "There was really no way to tell how successful he would be except I would say we all had a much better feeling about him than the rest of the country did, except for Mark Mangino. We were slightly taken aback that someone finally gave him a chance."

—◆—

Recruiting

*A*fter I won the 4A Player of the Year honors in Texas, I started getting some recruiting letters. But they were the letters that people send out for general information. They might have a questionnaire in them. But it was pretty much the letters they send out to people they might recruit — the letters that don't mean anything. A few coaches would drop by and watch our practices while they were out recruiting.

But by now I have started baseball, and at this point I am still thinking I am going to pursue baseball in college. Then I get the letter from Coach (Bill) Snyder, out of nowhere. It is a scholarship offer. I had not talked to a Kansas State coach on the phone to this point. I just opened up the letter, and it said, "You have been offered a full scholarship."

I thought, "Holy shit!" and I started freaking out that someone actually thought I could play football in college. It totally caught me off guard. When I had started getting the letters, I guess I thought OK, maybe there is a chance. Then all of a sudden to get the scholarship offer mid-spring your junior year ...

> **"I get the letter from Coach (Bill) Snyder. Out of nowhere, it is a scholarship offer. I had not talked to a Kansas State coach on the phone to this point. I just opened up the letter, and it said: "You have been offered a full scholarship."**

*"It did come out of the blue," Steve Reesing said. "I don't think
we had sent a tape, and we had not had any communication when
the letter arrived for a full scholarship.
We were thinking, 'Wow! How about this?'"*

—◆—

I called Coach Snyder and talked to him. He told me what he liked, and how I was elusive and made plays with my feet and all of those things. It came out of nowhere.

—◆—

*Snyder said, "Those letters were sent out to a very limited number
of people. Size was never a factor for us or we wouldn't have had
Darren Sproles or a whole bunch of other undersized guys that we had at
a number of positions. He was the kind of young person you like to have in
your program because he had leadership skills and many of the intrinsic
values that were significant to us. Our interest was strictly on what his
capabilities were and what kind of person he was."*

—◆—

Now I am playing baseball, but I am thinking I love football way more than baseball. And I was starting to kind of lose that passion for baseball. It wasn't active enough. I played outfield the year before, kind of waiting in turn to be the catcher. But my arm really wasn't holding up because of an elbow problem I had when I was young — basically tennis elbow.

So I said, "I'm done." My Dad said to give it another week. But after about five days, I said, "Coach, I am done, and I am just going to concentrate on football." That whole spring I just worked with my head coach, throwing weighted footballs to improve my arm strength, doing drops. All that stuff.

Except for talking to Coach Snyder, there weren't really any calls from coaches. How it went is that we, my Dad and I, were having to do most of the legwork. We were sending out highlight tapes and resumes to tons of schools — mostly schools that weren't the powerhouses. We figured the best chance was to go to a school that wasn't Texas or Texas A&M or Oklahoma. But anybody that was within range where it would be feasible, we were sending tapes.

Steve Reesing said, "We thought, especially after he won the award, that at this point in time schools were going to come calling. We assumed we would get a lot of interest and a lot of letters because you figure now that his name was known statewide that colleges would have him on a list. Nothing happened. I talked with Coach Dicus, and he basically told us that we needed to have a tape prepared so that if a college did call and say they wanted a tape, we would have one.

"When the season was over, I got copies of all his game tapes from the school, brought them home and one by one went through and picked out various plays. I took them to a local production company and put them all on one tape. During the spring, some of these schools started showing up at practice and expressing an interest. Duke came to Lake Travis High School, and there was a Purdue representative, a Northwestern representative. But most of them didn't seem all that serious."

— ◆ —

It's sort of funny because one of the conversations I had with a Texas A&M coach, he called late in May that year when they can start making contact again (following a recruiting dead period). He said, "Well, I like to be straight with guys, Todd. You know you are not one of the bigger or faster guys out there and maybe don't have the strongest arm. Right now you are on our B list of quarterbacks. But if things don't work out so well, maybe we could give you a look later on."

The whole time he is talking I am thinking, "I grew up a Longhorns fan, anyhow, so I am not coming to Aggieland." Sure enough I came down to A&M and we (Kansas) beat their asses. So I guess we know how that ends up.

I went to a camp at Baylor and threw. What's funny is that at the Baylor camp me and Case Keenan were both there along with a guy who ended up committing to Baylor. They didn't give me or Case a shot. He went to Houston and threw for 5,000-some yards last season. I think that is pretty funny now.

The first time I hear from a coach from Kansas, I was sitting in the airport waiting to fly up to Wichita to visit a buddy who had gone to Lake Travis before his family moved to Wichita. I was going to visit him for a day or two before I went to Kansas State's summer camp to see what Manhattan was like.

I heard from Coach (Tim) Beck, the guy who recruited me from Kansas, and he asked if I could send a tape. I said, "Yeah. I'll get one up there. Actually I am heading to Kansas right now to go to Wichita and then I go to the Kansas State camp."

The way my resume tape got to KU was that my Dad's college roommate — and my Godfather — was Tom Stotsman. His son married Pat Henderson's daughter. Pat used to be a coach and now works in the athletic office. So we passed the resume to Pat, and he got it over to Coach Mangino's staff.

So I go up to Wichita and then go to K-State's camp. I see Manhattan, and I am like, "Man this place isn't that nice." Obviously, beggars can't be choosers, but ...

Coach Snyder was still there. I got to talk to him and work with their quarterback coach a bunch while I was there. I did the whole camp. I was thinking, "This place is OK." But coming from Austin, the bar is set kind of high for cool places to live.

—◆—

Snyder said, "His intelligence for the game became very apparent, and he was good at receiver selection. He wasn't a young guy who would get rattled and forget about his progression. You would see his confidence as he would go from A to B to C to D. And he wasn't afraid to throw the ball."

—◆—

So after the camp, I drive on to Lawrence. I come into town and drive down Mass Street. It was a beautiful day during the summer. I was like, "This place is so much cooler than Manhattan." I was thinking, "I hope they offer me because I would much rather go here than to Kansas State. And plus, blue and red is a lot cooler than purple."

That's the kind of thing that a 17-year-old kid is thinking. So I am thinking about those things.

—◆—

Steve Reesing said, "We had finished up the Kansas State camp, and we were going to drive back to the airport. I called Coach Beck while we were in Manhattan, literally from outside the gym at K-State, and said, 'Hey, we're here in a camp, why don't we swing by and say hi to you guys while we're in Kansas?' So we literally just dropped in on them and met Coach Beck. He introduced us to Coach (Nick) Quartaro while we were there. Then they had us go on a tour of the campus. While we were there, I assume they all got together while we were on the campus tour. When we got back, that's when he brought in Coach Mangino."

—♦—

At this point, I don't know anything about the coach's history. I didn't know anything except that he was the coach. So for about 15 minutes, he was just shooting the shit with me and my Dad and my Mom — talking about football a little at the very end. But before that, he was talking about life in general and school and just anything, just having a good conversation.

Then toward the end of the conversation, he said, "You know, I watched your film yesterday. I like the way you make plays. You're real elusive ... can tell from talking to you that you carry yourself well, that you're a leader. I think I am going to go ahead and offer you a scholarship."

He had just watched the tape earlier that day or the day before. It had just gotten there. So I was like, "Really?" If my parents had not been there to try and say let's wait, I probably would have committed on the spot. That was enough for me. Coach Beck had told me that they were probably going to take two quarterbacks. A week or two later Tyler Lawrence committed. So I was thinking I had better go ahead and pull the trigger because I don't want some other kid to commit and I am left out in the dark with no other offers.

—♦—

Mangino said, "His tape was hard to ignore. I watched it with a couple of guys on the offense and we said, 'Holy Cow! This guy is making plays all over the place.' He came in and was really small. What convinced me was he shook my hand, and looked me in the eye. He was intelligent and a very confident guy. He could speak on subjects other than just football. He had a little bounce to him. He exuded confidence, and he was just like a stick of dynamite. I remember going down the hall when he was out taking a tour of the campus, and the coaches said, 'What do you think?' I said, 'He's small, but I like him. We are going to offer him a scholarship.'"

—♦—

Steve Reesing said, "What attracted Todd — and there are more stories as we went to other schools — was that Coach Mangino didn't beat around the bush. We were there a short amount of time, and he immediately came and said, 'You are a player. I like what I see in your tape. I don't care that you are small because you don't need to be big to run my offense.' Those are the words you want to hear."

— ◆ —

After KU, I ended up going to a camp at Purdue, a camp at Duke, Baylor ... Duke offered me, but I had to fly out to freaking North Carolina and throw in front of them to convince Duke to offer me a scholarship. I went to their camp a couple of weeks later, but I got back and said my mind is made up. I called and committed, and then I didn't have to worry about anything my whole senior year. It was a nice thing to not have to worry about recruiting.

I could have waited around, and maybe after my senior year I would have gotten some more interest. But I didn't really know.

At all the camps, everyone brought up my size. I was always the shortest quarterback at any of the camps. But I would be there, and I am throwing just as good or better than these other guys who are there, then why the hell aren't they giving me a scholarship offer? I knew I was short, but I am thinking, "What is the big freaking deal? OK, so I am a little bit shorter. But I have proven I can play quarterback. Look at my stats!"

But it came up every time. I was at a TCU camp, and we were going through drills. I was throwing the ball fine. But I over-stride on a throw. I hear, "Reesing! Come here! What are you doing? You can't be doing that." He asked how tall I was, I said, "I don't know, 5' 11" or so." He goes on, "When you over-stride, you are 5'4". You can't afford to do that."

I am thinking, "If you don't like it, then tell me to get out of here because, personally, I am not digging your style either."

Dicus said, "There were a lot of coaches in for spring ball the year prior to his senior year. They were coming by carloads watching him, and we had a receiver and a running back. But that was the biggest question: 'Can he play with that height at the D-1 level?' Some coaches were very concerned about it. Certain coaches have their own philosophy and the type of quarterback they want height-wise. I remember Purdue was pretty high on him, there was just that question mark. Once Todd committed to Kansas, they kind of regretted not getting him."

—◆—

I went by Northwestern, went by Purdue. Everywhere I went, people could only talk about my size. Even Purdue. I talked to the offensive coordinator about Drew Brees and how he was there and he wasn't that much bigger than I am. I think they were probably more OK with it, but they were still hesitant. I never even got to talk to the head coach.

—◆—

Steve Reesing said, "After we went through the trip to Duke and Purdue and Northwestern — all the schools that had shown an interest in the spring — we sat down and evaluated it. We have an offer from K-State, an offer from KU and, as a result of that trip, we got an offer from Duke. Northwestern and Purdue had no intention of offering after he worked out for them. At all of them, Todd was completely out-throwing all the other kids. Every time, you had all these tall skinny kids throwing the football. Todd was always the shortest of the group, but his arm was stronger than any of them."

—◆—

There weren't any throws that were a real problem. Compared to most of the guys I was throwing with, I had pretty good velocity. You learn when you get to college that you don't always have to throw it as hard as you can. But at the camps, everyone tries to throw it really hard. There were some guys who had pretty strong arms, but no one out there made me look like I didn't deserve to be out there throwing.

I am shaking my head. "I don't get it. I don't see what the big deal is." But you learn real fast, everyone wants the size. They want somebody who looks like a thoroughbred instead of a guy who runs like Seabiscuit, I guess.

But Coach Mangino, he came into the room wearing one of those Hawaiian shirts that he always wore. He said, "I know some people say you are shorter and not big enough to play or this and that. I know you are a small guy. I see how big you are. But that doesn't matter to me. If I think a guy can play football ... I have seen what you can do and make plays, then that is fine with me."

He basically, unlike anyone else, just dispelled the fact that my size was a problem. He said, "I saw a guy who can play football on film. I like him as a person. That's good enough for me."

—◆—

Jake Sharp, KU's size-challenged tailback at 5'10", says that's one of the best things about Mangino. "My first Todd Reesing experience, we were both in high school and came up to a game. I got introduced to him at the recruit tent, and he said, 'I am Todd, and I am a quarterback.' I looked at him like, 'Are you serious? I'm an undersized running back, and I am looking you eye to eye. OK, cool.' You really have to give Coach Mangino credit. He is one of those guys who looks for football players. He didn't look at just the numbers and stuff."

—◆—

So the whole recruiting process happened really fast. From getting that first offer in maybe March or so from Coach Snyder, to committing basically at the beginning of July. I went to a bunch of camps in June, a bunch of visits to different schools. I only took one official visit, the one to Kansas.

I committed because of what I was hearing from everybody and how different meeting with Coach Mangino was and his automatically bestowing confidence on me by saying, "I don't care what your size is, I think you can play. I think you can play for us." No one else was saying that and I didn't want to risk waiting to see if someone else might offer in the future.

I mean, this guy sounds like he is going to give me a fair chance. I loved Lawrence right away. I said I didn't see any reason for a need to wait. It seemed like a pretty good deal to me. It was in the Big 12, which was appealing. You have a chance to play all those different schools and go back and prove them all wrong.

——◆——

Dicus said, "Short is less of a factor in high school. It never ever crossed our minds about his height. The competitor that Todd had in him, going into a game we knew we had a chance of winning because we had him at the helm. If you just put the ball in his hands, he was going to make things happen — whether it be him in the pocket and throwing or whether it was him escaping and making things happen either with his arm or his feet.

——◆——

"Coach Mangino up there at Kansas gave him an opportunity, and he proved people wrong, showed them that his height wasn't an issue. If you put the ball in his hands, because of his understanding of offenses and defenses and his ability to make plays, he is going to take you where you want to go."

——◆——

Todd Reesing signing his letter of intent to play at KU, flanked by (l-r) Lake Travis offensive coordinator Jerry Bird, athletic director Jack Moss, and head coach Jeff Dicus.

Debi Reesing said, "He just wanted a chance. It's kind of like his high school coach learned and Coach Mangino learned. If you unleash Todd, he will find a way to get the job done. He is not one of those OK, that-receiver-is-covered-so-I-will-throw-the-ball-out-of-bounds quarterbacks. Uh-uh. That's not the way Todd thinks."

— ◆ —

Early enrollment

I wanted to graduate early from Lake Travis so I could go to KU for spring ball and conditioning. Not many guys were doing that at the time. But I thought it would give me a chance to be competitive and maybe play when I was a freshman.

But Lake Travis changed their schedule my senior year, so I had to take classes at three different places to get all my credits in. We had been on the block schedule, where you would take four classes in the fall and four in the spring. And if they had stayed with that, I would have graduated. But I don't think the school wanted people leaving after the first semester. So they changed it. You still had your eight classes, but you would take them the whole year.

I think two classes I needed were just half-year classes, so I could take them normally like I would. But I had to take English 4, which was a class you would normally take a full year. I took that through Texas Tech online. The other class I took was an economics class through Austin Community College that I did at night on Tuesdays.

So my parents knew that's what I was doing because the whole fall we were talking about having to get ready to go here and there to get to the classes.

— ◆ —

Debi Reesing said, "Todd was always, to me, a little mature beyond his years. He had gone to his high school counselor, unbeknownst to us, and he figured out how to do the scheduling and how to take the courses at three different places to graduate in December so he could go early. When he sat us down and talked to us about it, he was really adult and presented his course of action. It was kind of a shock because you think about spring of your senior year. But he wasn't playing baseball any more, and by then the prom thing is old.

"It was kind of bittersweet, obviously. You think you have time to prepare yourself for that separation. Although he had given it lots of thought and had numerous visits with his high school counselor about it, he sort of sprung it on us in December. So in a way it was a little quick. But you know, that's kind of Todd's quick decision-making, too."

— ◆ —

They wanted me to have a chance to play somewhere. They obviously wanted me to go to a school that had good academics. My mom was really big on that. She wouldn't let me go just anywhere. I had lived in Austin all my life, and a lot of my friends were thinking of going to college outside of Austin. I was excited about going somewhere new and meeting new people in a different place in the country. Everything about it was exciting, starting with a whole new crowd of people and a whole new lifestyle.

My parents didn't really take any convincing. They were ecstatic I was getting a chance to play football, and they wanted me to put my best foot forward for that.

— ◆ —

Steve Reesing said, "I think he was ready to graduate from high school, emotionally and academically. We thought it was a great idea to go there and go through spring practice and get him off to start his next adventure. He was mentally ready to move on from high school."

— ◆ —

First Game

CHAPTER 5

'Coach wants to talk to you.'

"Coach Mangino wants to talk to you."

"Hey, Coach, what's going on? You wanted to see me?"

"Hey, Todd, how you feeling?"

"I'm good, just hanging out."

"Well, we're going to go ahead and start you the second half."

What? I'm trying to hold back, but I'm thinking, "Holy shit! Is he kidding me?"

There was a little less than a minute left in the first half of our ninth game of the year. I was redshirting behind Kerry Meier and Adam Barmann. I didn't think there was any way I was going to see the field at this point in the season.

Coach said, "I just want you to go out there and have fun. You don't have to worry about us pulling you out of the game or worry about looking over your shoulder. Go out there, have fun, do what you do, and make plays."

I was like, "Yes, sir." Then he said, "Let's put it this way: You can't do any worse."

The week before, Coach had asked me if they had to pull my redshirt off if I would be OK with that. I said, "Yeah. Whatever. If you need me to play, I'll be ready to go." I certainly wasn't going to say no. I'm thinking, "Get me in a game if there is any chance." But I had talked to some of the older guys and they were all saying, "Naw, man, there is no way they will burn your redshirt this late in the season. You don't have to worry about playing."

Now I have about 15 minutes before achieving my dream of quarterbacking a Division I football team ... and it's in a game in which our offense had just been dismal in the first half. I think we had like 90 yards of offense, and it had been painful to watch. Kerry wasn't playing because he was hurt. So Adam was on the field, but it wasn't Adam. That wouldn't be fair to him. No one was doing anything. So I guess Coach figured let's try to spark it somehow. That's how my first nickname "Sparky" came about. He started calling me "Sparky" from when I sparked the offense that first game.

So now we're going in for halftime, and I haven't done a dead sprint or live action or anything except stand on the sidelines with my ball cap on and signal in the plays. Between series I would watch, just like always. I hadn't even broken a sweat, really, hadn't run a bit or even thrown a ball. So I'm thinking I better get stretched out at halftime.

I'm in there really working at it when Adam walks into the locker room. He comes over and says: "Todd, are you going in?"

I was like, "Yeah, didn't they tell you?"

Adam was a great guy. He was the guy who really took me in and mentored me a lot that first spring I was there at school and helped teach me the offense. He could have been really upset, but he was like, "OK, man. Let's go get 'em." He was real supportive, and it meant a lot to me to see that he was not getting really upset.

—◆—

Steve and Debi Reesing, Todd's parents, hadn't made the trip to Lawrence for the Colorado game. Steve said, "We were shocked. I remember I had gone to the Lake Travis game on Friday night before the Colorado game. We had made some of the KU games, but we had decided not to go to that one. But Kerry was hurt, and I couldn't get my mind off it. I couldn't stand it, so I went behind the stands at game time on Friday night and called Todd on my cell phone: 'Now, Todd, are you sure it's going to be OK that we are not going to be at this football game tomorrow? I am prepared to jump on a plane tomorrow morning and be there.'

"He said: 'No, no, no, Dad, don't worry about it. This is the ninth game of the year. They are not going to pull my redshirt now.' I went, 'OK, I just wanted to make sure and check because I sure would not want to miss you playing.' The game wasn't on TV or the radio where we could get it."

—◆—

I had run all the second-team reps that week since Kerry was out. So I had been running the plays, doing the game plan and all that stuff. That week wasn't like all the others when I stood on the sideline and signaled in the plays. So at least I knew the plays and knew what was going on.

—◆—

Kyle Reesing said, "I know he was probably nervous in that game, but in his whole life, Todd never backed down from anything. I know from talking to him, his attitude was, 'OK, let's do this!' Basically that was all it took for him to get his mental focus ready. Just come and play your game, and things will happen. He has confidence, and that's a very good thing for an athlete. If you don't believe in yourself, you are not going to be successful. So you have to believe in your talent. That's something Todd has always had."

—◆—

The first action

We come out for the second half and I am so amped up you can't believe it. We're getting the ball to open the second half, and I remember the PA announcer saying: "Now at quarterback, No. 5 ... " I think people were excited about seeing some sort of change in any way.

The first play we just hand off. We are playing a normal formation, and I am under center. They want me to get a snap and not have those crazy jitters. Everything goes fine. Jon Cornish runs for a 5-yard gain.

Next play, we try to do a little rollout from the same kind of formation. I come away from center, and this (defensive) guy is right in my face. I am freaked out, jump back and throw the ball incomplete. That kind of woke me up and made me realize that this was for real. I don't think I got hit, maybe just shoved a little bit.

So the next play, I get back in the shotgun to throw the ball. We're running slants to try and get a first down. At this point, things are just flying around me. Everything is going really fast. I get the snap, and of course for my first real pass in college I am staring down the receiver. I try to throw it to Dexton Fields. The linebacker can see in my eyes exactly where I am going to throw it. He goes over, tips it, and it's intercepted.

My first real pass is intercepted. We've already thrown two interceptions in the game. I come in there, and I want to spark the team and want to do well, and "Boom!" I throw an interception, just like that. I am thinking, "You have got to be freaking kidding me! Just throw it incomplete. Anything, just don't throw an interception." As I get to the sidelines everyone is really good. All the guys are coming up and saying, "Just calm down. You're good." Adam is the first one over there saying, "Hey, don't worry about it." Then he's asking what did I see, talks through it with me, this and that.

—◆—

Colorado coach Dan Hawkins remembers Reesing's entrance into the game, "The feeling on our sideline was that they were raising the white flag, and I said, 'Let's not be so sure. If it's me and I'm trotting out a true freshman out there and taking off his redshirt, I'm not raising the white flag.'"

—◆—

The defense held, thankfully, and when I go out for the second series, things have slowed down a little bit. I am trying to not think about the interception. We run the ball again. Then I run it and get tackled for the first time. Then I complete my first pass to Brian Murphy for 5 yards and a first down. We moved the ball a little bit but ended up stalling out.

The third series we come out and on a play-action pass from under center, I hit Jake Sharp down the sideline on that wheel route we ran so often. He runs for like 47 yards. When I pulled up and threw that ball Jake hadn't turned around yet. I'm thinking, "Just turn around and catch the ball, Jake!" He finally did, and at that point I knew we were going to start clicking.

Sharp said, "The one thing I remember from that game is that Todd and I had basically our coming out party together. That was a wheel route to me. It was like the first big connection we ever had."

— ♦ —

That was the biggest play that had happened in the game to that point. Once I hit that first big play and people were yelling, then I kind of went, "Whew!" I think I took my first deep breath and thought I could relax a little bit.

Once you play those first two or three series you realize:

A. You are not going to die when they hit you.

B. It is moving fast but not that much faster than you remember.

I had been in some scrimmages here and there, but they never really hit you. In games they are not pulling off of you. So you have to remember that. In practice, guys are pulling up. Once you get hit once, throw the first pass, throw the first interception, you can sort of say, "I have gone through everything, now let's just go back and play." It's important to run with the ball that first time and get tackled. It kind of releases that built-up energy because you are so amped up, and your adrenaline is pumping. You want to run the ball and do all this stuff. To get hit it kind of brings you back to earth and you can calm down. But that usually happens in the first game or two, not in the ninth game of the year.

> **"Once you play those first two or three series you realize:
> A. You are not going to die when they hit you.
> B. It is moving fast but not that much faster than you remember."**

Once I hit that first big play, then I hit a little slip screen to Jon Cornish, who ran it in for a touchdown for our first score of the game. At that point, you have hit kind of two big plays in a short period of time. That is when the smile came back on my face and I thought, "Now this is what I know."

We hit that score at the end of the third quarter, and we get the ball right back when Aqib Talib intercepts it and takes it back to Colorado's 24. So we're back and we start moving the ball again. I scramble for a 14-yard gain on the first play, and danged if I don't freaking fumble the ball. Fortunately, Anthony Collins fell on it at the 8. Cornish gains 5, then I throw an incomplete pass. Now we line up in the shotgun on a third down. That's when I get my first touchdown on a 3-yard run.

That whole game just went really fast. There was one play that sort of typifies what was racing through my mind the whole game. We're in the shotgun with a Ringo protection, which means the running back is set to my right. I look at the field, and they are rolling the coverage to a single safety and they're going to blitz off the edge. I know the protections somewhat, but not all that well. But I do know there is no one blocking this guy who is going to blitz. My mind starts racing. "What the hell! What am I supposed to call? How do I fix this? What am I supposed to do?"

I look at the play clock, it is winding down, so I just think, "Forget it." I'm just going to say: "Hut!" I'll just have to make him miss. It's one on one. I like my chances with any blitzing linebacker in that situation. He blitzes. I make him miss and look like an idiot. He falls down. I get away. So the plan works.

That's the play I end up hitting Jeff Foster on a deep pass down the left side of the field for 31 yards. It's another big drive that we finish off with a touchdown to Derek Fine. We score three times in a row, making it a 21-point swing, and now we're up 21-9 and people are wondering what just happened.

———◆———

Sharp said Reesing was on top of his game. "The funny thing about that is that as a freshman, I really had no idea what I was doing out there. On the big play we had, I lined up and Todd is starting the cadence. I look over at him and go, 'Hey, is this the wheel route to me?' He goes, 'Yes! Set! Hut!' and I take off running. It all worked out well, but it was really hilarious. We both were just out there winging it. There were several times that happened when we were youngsters."

———◆———

The next drive we have a third down, and I am in the shotgun. We have a double slant concept to a three-receiver side. I catch it and get ready to throw. I felt there was a linebacker watching so he could waltz through and intercept it. So I stopped. Instead of throwing to the left, I came down and looked to the right to start running.

Sometimes people will ask how I scramble or what I was thinking. I don't know, I am just reacting, trying not to get hit. I don't know why I take off in certain directions. I have no idea.

So I take off right, get a block, cut back left, go up field. Literally, it is back and forth, and all of a sudden I catch myself breaking open with no one in front of me — just the end zone about 40 yards away. So I start running as fast as I can. Now, I had just run 50 yards from side to side to get 20 yards down the field, but I am thinking this would be amazing if I get into the end zone.

But a guy starts catching me. The defensive back was a lot faster than the guy who had been standing around nine weeks with a clipboard in his hands. He starts running me down. I am running out of breath. The guy is catching me, and I know I am not going to beat him to the pylon. So I try to cut back and maybe he'll run past me. He ends up tackling me at the 1. It's kind of funny that the longest run I ever had was in the first game I ever played.

So now we want to quick-snap them. Next play we try to line up and get a play off really quickly. Someone jumps off sides. I wish we hadn't tried to quick-snap them because we would have scored. Now, instead of a touchdown, we have the penalty and I come back and make the worst play of the game, possibly the worst play of my career.

I'm still tired from the long run, but they call a quarterback draw. I get the ball, step back and then take off to the left. As I cut, I make the cardinal error, let my arm raise up and let the ball get exposed. Guy hits it. The ball pops up right in front of me. I see it, but I am kind of off balance, and I get hit as I try to jump toward the ball. As I reached out, I got absolutely helicoptered, and I am flying parallel to the ground. I watch the safety take the ball full speed. When I finally hit the ground, this guy has taken off 90 yards for a touchdown that cuts the lead to five points.

I am thinking, "You have got to be kidding me. I just ran 63 yards, I am still out of breath and now I give them a touchdown that essentially puts them back in the game." If I do all this and come back and blow it that sure would suck. Luckily, they tried an onside kick that we recovered and ran some time off the clock. Even though they got a Hail Mary pass for 61 yards on the final play of the game, we hung on for the win.

But that whole game was just flying by. Everything was happening so fast on the field. On the blitzes, we had simple calls that would take care of it. But I just blanked it out of my mind. When I was looking at coverages, I would look up and have absolutely no idea of what coverage they were playing. I didn't know what their defensive front was. I didn't know if they were blitzing some of the time.

If they blitzed or something didn't go well, it was like, "You know what, I will just have to make a play." The whole game I was winging it. I was literally going up there and saying, "Hut."

—◆—

Hawkins said, "He about single-handedly won that football game.
He made some great plays. From my perspective it was like,
Holy Cow! Where did that guy come from? We were a part of
his coming out party as a freshman."

—◆—

I think it was the only game I played that my parents didn't see. There was no reason for them to be going to the games that year because I was a redshirt. It was so unlikely that I was going to play that friends told me they were leaving the game after halftime, literally walking out of the stadium when the announcer came on and said, "Now playing quarterback, No. 5, Todd Reesing." They turned right back around and went into the stadium to watch the second half.

—◆—

Debi Reesing, Todd's mother, was outside talking to
neighbors in their cul-de-sac at Bee Cave, Texas, when Todd went into the
game. "Steve came running out the front door and he goes, 'Oh my gosh!
You will never believe it. They just pulled Todd's redshirt and sent

him into the game!' The whole cul-de-sac started cheering and applauding. We were tracking the game on the internet, which was really slow and pretty unsatisfying how they used the little football field of where the ball is. I was running out the door giving everybody updates.
"Some of Todd's friends from KU called during the game. They were saying, 'Listen to the crowd. He has energized the crowd.' Others called after the game. We were so proud of him, and that was actually kind of a special moment. Even though we weren't there, all his friends called from KU and made it special."

—◆—

Looking back, I guess it is bad I didn't tell them to come because they missed the first game I played in. They haven't missed one since. But I'm glad they pulled the redshirt off. I would have still had another year in 2010 if they hadn't. But if they hadn't, I might not have gotten a real chance to compete the next spring.

—◆—

"I think about that sometimes," said KU athletic director Lew Perkins, a huge Reesing fan. "Selfishly, I wish we would have had him for another year. But we might not have had that wonderful season if he hadn't gotten on the field."

—◆—

We would have gone into spring ball and there would have been no reason for them to open up the quarterback competition. They would have had a guy (Kerry Meier) who played the whole year and who everyone thinks is going to be a great quarterback — which he probably would have.

I would not have played in a game, ever. So of course they would not have made it a competition. But because I played and showed I could make plays when I was out there, I got a fair shot. We have a new offensive coordinator coming in, and it's a full-fledged competition. Kerry still probably had a foot forward because he's started a bunch of games, had won games and he had made plays. People still thought he was their guy.

Me, I'm thinking this is all I want, a chance to compete for the job.

Adrian Mayes, a left guard who would start in the 2007
and 2008 seasons, said, "I wasn't surprised he was able to do that,
which is sort of funny to say. But a lot of the guys knew that eventually he
was going to take over. He had already earned himself a nickname
called 'Sparky' before he even played a game. He always, even in
practice, would provide a spark to the offense."

—◆—

Linebacker James Holt said, "Just by the way he went
into the Colorado game you could see he was a confident guy.
He just knows how to play the game. He was the same the whole
season, confident and ready to go out and play."

—◆—

I had kind of accepted my role up to that point because there wasn't really a whole lot I could do about it. It was Kerry's job, and I didn't have a chance to sway that. I had kind of started to get acclimated to that in spring ball when I am getting less reps. Kerry was strictly first team. All you were hearing was "Kerry is the next great quarterback. He is going to be the savior. "I was thinking, "Cool, but when do I get to play, you know?" That whole idea didn't sound like it had a whole lot of playing time for me involved.

Not playing is tough. That's what a lot of kids coming in their first year have trouble with. Everyone who comes to college, at their high school they were the man. They were most likely the best player on their team. Then you come to college and you are bogged down in the pecking order. You have older guys who aren't going to be your best friend right away. They are here to win ballgames.

So as the season started, I fell into my role. I would go out and do the warm-up at practice, throw some routes to receivers. Then once we started seven-on-seven and game-planning stuff, I was over on the sidelines next to one of the managers.

I was the one who signaled in the plays during the games, so that's what I was doing the whole practice. Coach wanted it to be more like a game and make the signals crisp. At that point I thought there was no way I was going to play.

Kyle Reesing said, "I don't think he was frustrated because when you know you are redshirting, the mentality of that is that you do everything you can to get better and help your team — whether it is on the practice squad or whatever. So he wasn't frustrated by that because they told him from the get-go they were planning to redshirt him. But after he led them back in the Colorado game, he played sparingly in the next three games. That was the frustrating part of that season to him. His attitude was, 'OK, you just burned my redshirt, and I showed you I can play. So why aren't you playing me?' He felt it was a kind of 'We sort of believe in your attitude' and that fueled him in the off-season because he wanted to go out there to prove to the coaches that he could be the guy."

—◆—

Winning the Job **6** CHAPTER

For most fans, the 2007 season began with our first game against Central Michigan. I learned I was going to be the starter about two weeks before that game. But I had been working for months before I learned I would be the starting quarterback.

It was such a relief to finally get the word from Coach Mangino because then I could start working on being a leader of our team rather that worrying about trying to impress the coaches with every play you get in practice. It's a completely different mindset.

Spring practice

After getting a small taste of playing in my freshman season, I was determined to come back and give it my best shot to win the starting job this year. After the Colorado game, I really didn't get to play much. Kerry was back (from injury), and they had him start. I am not going to lie. That sucked a little bit. I figured, they just pulled my redshirt. I helped bring us back in a game — it wasn't all me, but we got a win. We were still in contention to be bowl eligible, and I had helped in a way to keep the dreams alive for a bowl game. And I didn't even get to start. I got to play, but the Colorado game was the only game where I was a substantial contributor, and that was only for one half.

So I come back in January, and I am anxious to get back into the routine of things. Coach (Nick) Quartaro, who had been the offensive coordinator and quarterbacks coach, had decided to leave football and move on. So there was going to be a new offensive coordinator, and that was huge for me.

Coach Quartaro had recruited Kerry. He had been the one mentoring Kerry and bringing him along. Kerry had started a bunch of games, had won games, had made a lot of plays. Who wouldn't like him? He's a great athlete, 6'3", can run and throw. A lot of people still thought he was their guy.

Me, I'm thinking all I want is a chance to compete for the job. When the new OC comes in, and any time you have a new system, a new OC and a new quarterback coach, there's probably going to be some competition unless you have a guy who has been all conference for two years or something.

So when spring practice comes around, it was anybody's job. Kerry probably had a slight foot forward. But I thought I would at least get a chance. That's why the decision from the year before was so important when they pulled my redshirt off. If I hadn't played that game in Colorado and showed I could make some plays, why would they have opened up the competition? They would have already had a guy who played the whole year, and I would not have ever played in a game.

Then Coach (Ed) Warinner was hired. I have no idea who he is. I had heard some things from some of the offensive linemen because he had been the offensive line coach at KU two years before and had left for Illinois. So he comes in, and I hear from the older guys — mostly the O-Line — that he's a stern, in-your-face guy. He's loud. He's a yeller. He wants things done his way. Offensive linemen have to deal with that a lot.

I am thinking, "OK, that doesn't bother me. My old high school coach used to get in my grill, too." So Coach Warinner comes in, and we start hearing about the new system. It's going to be no-huddle with a lot of shotgun. At first it wasn't going to be all shotgun because we had a good tight end, good offensive linemen, good solid running back and good fullback. So we were still going to go under center.

But there was going to be a lot of shotgun to spread teams out. As soon as I find that out, I think, that's good because it's more like what I ran in high school.

Adrian Mayes, who would win a starting left guard spot in spring practice, said, "Todd pretty much took charge the first time that offense was put in place. They were having a competition, but in the back of everybody's mind, we all knew that Todd would be the quarterback. Kerry, being a good quarterback and a great athlete himself, they would find another position for him to play. But Todd pretty much took charge from the get-go, and I knew he would be the starting quarterback."

—◆—

Coach Warinner and Coach Mangino let us know it was an open competition and we had to earn it by playing well, showing leadership as a quarterback, yada, yada, yada, the list everyone says when there is a quarterback competition.

So spring starts, and it's back and forth. Kerry is usually taking the first set of snaps with the first team, which kind of meant that he was a little ahead. He started out being the first-teamer, and I was a little behind. But we would rotate after that. At the beginning, it kind of felt like he had the jump start because he had started the prior season, had a lot of playing experience and he was older by a year.

So I know that every snap I have, every play, I am being watched. Every play was a competition. I have to prove myself every time. I know I am getting a chance because the reps were pretty even. But I know I have to really make the most of them. I can't afford to have a bad practice. I took the approach that if I had a bad practice or even a bad play, then it's going to hurt my chances of winning the job. I can't afford any bad days.

> **"I can't afford any bad days."**

It wasn't like Kerry and I were looking at each other like we wanted the other one to do bad. It wasn't that at all. My focus was just that I had to do well. I was more focused about me. I knew Kerry was going to do well. So I knew I had to do really well to do better than he was going to do.

—◆—

Running back Jake Sharp, who also had played as a true freshman, saw the competition up close and personal, "When we came in for the spring, it was kind of like, 'Wow, Todd and Kerry are really even.' Come the fall, they were really even. But with the style of offense Coach Warinner wanted to run and with Coach Warinner's personality, Todd fit it better. I think Todd just clicked with him."

—◆—

All spring, it was back and forth. He would have some really good days. I would have some really good days. We both played pretty dang well in the spring scrimmage, both threw touchdowns, had big plays. It was like that the whole spring.

So it's pretty dead even. No one is ahead, everybody is making plays. Because we both did really well in the spring game, it became pretty clear they wouldn't be able to announce a starter at the end of spring practice.

Everybody around is buzzing: Some guys, "I think it should be him." Others, "No, I think it should be him." The media was saying it should be this guy or that guy, yada, yada, yada. They're all trying to list their reasons like they know because they have been out there at practice. So they are thinking they should know who should be starting. People have no idea what's going on. But it gives them something to talk about on the blogs or whatever.

So we finish out the spring and do the summer program. Both of us work hard. We both get in good shape. We're strong. We're fast. Whatever. But we both knew that no one was going to win the job in the summer. So we kept doing our reps, switching off like we did all spring long — splitting time. We knew it was going to come down to two-a-days, full pads.

Two-a-days

So we get to August. The season is around the corner. We're in full pads now. The coaches are starting to put more pressure on us, and every play is that much more important. In spring ball, you can make some mistakes, as we both were with the new offense. And that first spring Coach Warinner was in our faces all the time. He wanted things done exactly his way. He was constantly yelling, and he yelled at me and Kerry more than anybody else on the rest of the team. He knew that if he could get us two to do things the right way, then everyone else would follow suit.

So I got yelled at more in that first spring ball by Coach Warinner than I have been yelled at the entire rest of my football career. But both of us caught on, and he stopped yelling at me and

Kerry after the first year. Then he started yelling at the running backs or offensive line or receivers. But once he got us doing things the right way, he let off.

Kerry and I were living together at the time. We would get home at night and sit down. We didn't talk football too much, it was more like, "Man, dude. He yells a lot." We were laughing about it.

But we never really talked about the competition. We would talk about practice and other people and how things happened. And if one of us had made a sweet play, the other would say so. We both wanted the other guy to do well, then at the end let the best man win.

Of course, I thought I would win. I am sure he thought he would win, too.

So the competition is wide open when we start two-a-days. Then things start getting really intense. Every play is important. You don't want to make mistakes, but you have to make plays to stand out. When I would scramble, I didn't want to force a throw and throw an interception and show I was making bad decisions and turning the ball over. That's not what they want at all. But at the same time, you have to push the envelope to make plays and show them, "This is what I am going to do in the game, and this is why I should win the job."

So it's a balance of being smart and also kind of playing your game.

Then Kerry's hamstring starts to hamper him a little bit. It had started right at the end of the summer, and it bothers him. It never really hurt, but it always kind of bothered him — like my groin has for the last four or five months. It never really heals because you are still pushing hard in practices every day.

So about the second week of two-a-days, I started to pull ahead. I was making plays. I had really gotten back into my game. After about the first 10 practices or so, I started to feel like it was my job. We were still switching off, but I was starting to get the sense that … I just kind of felt like the guys on the team felt it was my job. I was making plays, and they were having to worry about Kerry rehabbing his hamstring — which wasn't helping his chances, especially since he had just been hurt a whole bunch the season before.

KU tight end Derek Fine sensed the shift as well. "Even going back to the spring, he came into that spring with kind of more of an attitude, not cocky but confident. The thing Todd had a little bit over Kerry that you could see in the spring is that whenever Todd would get flushed out of the pocket, he would always have his eyes downfield to see a receiver to throw it to. His idea was to throw it first, run second. I mean, he was a little guy. I wouldn't want to be running into those big cats, either. Kerry is a big, athletic, really fast guy. When he would get flushed from the pocket, his first natural instinct was to tuck the ball — more run first and throw second. "I think that is what kind of gave Todd the upper hand with the new offensive coordinator. That was something Coach Warinner really liked."

—◆—

Mayes said, "Todd can make plays that aren't there. Both guys were mobile guys, and Kerry could make plays, too. But when Todd was making plays with his feet, he was always using his feet to throw the ball downfield, not necessarily to take off and run or anything."

—◆—

They brought me in about two weeks before the season started and said Coach was going to announce me as the starter.

—◆—

At the time of the announcement, Coach Mangino said, "The best way to put it is Reesing came out of the blocks ready to go. He had a great deal of retention from last spring. He showed good presence in the pocket, handled the huddle very well. We have known for a while that it was going to be him, but we wanted to wait. We decided about two weeks out (from the first game) we'd make a public comment."

—◆—

I remember talking about it in the interviews what a relief it was to finally get that announcement. Then I didn't have to look over my shoulder every practice. I didn't have to worry that every throw

Todd and former KU tight end Derek Fine.

was being judged. You still had to prove yourself every day, but I could kind of relax and focus more on being a leader on the offense and work on my fundamentals and learn more. Then you allow yourself to relax and work more on understanding things instead of worrying about making mistakes and the competition to win the job.

Leadership responsibilities

Even though it was only my second year and there were a bunch of seniors who had been there for five years like Derek (Fine), and David Ochoa and Brandon McAnderson, it was still my job to be the leader. I am the voice of the offense. I am the guy who, if we had a huddle, would command the huddle. They are looking to me.

Coach Warinner always said if everyone else has a bad practice, but the quarterback has a great practice, overall it is not a bad practice. But whenever you have a bad practice, regardless of if everyone else looks great, it is going to be a bad practice. So you have the responsibility to show up every day and be ready to have a good practice. If you don't practice well, if you are not enthusiastic and talking on the sidelines and getting guys to stay focused and have fun, practice is going to be shitty. Coaches are going to yell more. You are going to get yelled at more.

—◆—

Mayes said, "His personality has a lot to do with it. He is one of those guys who was always vocal, always telling the wide receivers what to do and telling the offensive line good job and stuff like that. You know, congratulating everybody, making everybody feel good."

—◆—

Debi Reesing said, "Because Todd, with his size, has always had to play beyond himself in some respect, I think he is just a very fiery leader who pumps kids up and gets them going."

—◆—

If a quarterback is not prepared, it all leads to them. If you are an offensive lineman or receiver and you come in and maybe you don't have your best day, it is not noticed as much. If you miss a block or two, maybe it is not noticed on that play. Not run a great route, and you don't get thrown to. If there's anything I do bad on a play, then everybody knows. If I don't practice well, if I am not enthusiastic, if

I'm not talking, then everybody around me is not going to be as up for practice. That, in turn, makes it not as good of a practice.

—◆—

Perkins said, "I was never in the huddle, but I would imagine whenever he was in the huddle he had everybody's attention. In a crazy way, and this is probably unfair, his size probably had something to do with his confidence. I think he felt like he always had to prove himself because he was a small quarterback and not the fastest quarterback. He had to acquire other attributes to make him better."

—◆—

A new mindset

When you don't know if you are the starter, you are worrying, "I have two reps before he comes in, and I need to make the most of them." Afterwards, you are thinking, "All right. Let's figure out what's going on. Let's try to get better. Don't take chances. Let's move the chains." It's a different mindset. You don't have as much pressure on you. You don't get as upset when you make a mistake because you know you are not going to lose the job if you accidentally throw an interception on a mistake.

You can take a whole different approach to practice than when you are competing with someone who is just as good as you are at the position and when every play is a huge indicator of what your coaches are looking at. So for the rest of two-a-days, I could kind of focus on getting ready to be the guy for the team.

Then we come out in the first game and just crushed it.

—◆—

Fine said, "You could see his confidence evolve. When you are in the huddle, there is one guy everyone is looking at. You don't want to see any hesitancy from your quarterback, and I had been seeing that for years at KU. But that was one thing Todd never had, never ever. If he messed up, he was always, 'OK, I messed up this series, next series I am going to come out and throw a touchdown.' That rubs off on other players. When your quarterback is feeling good, that resonates with everyone, and we all play with confidence. That was a real positive thing that he brought, even just being a sophomore and 20 years old."

—◆—

I'm sure Kerry was disappointed because he's as much of a competitor as I am. Of course he was frustrated because he wanted to win. But he was always there supporting me, and he accepted the fact I had proven I was deserving of the job. I would think a guy like Kerry, he was more upset with himself. That's how I would have been.

——◆——

Meier said, "To tell you the truth, the initial blow when I talked to Coach Mangino and Coach Warinner, the initial blow definitely hurt. I won't sit here and tell you I didn't mind it or anything like that. But I knew that in the short time I had known Todd, and knew what we had off the field as far as being friends was much more important than our situation and relationship on the field.

"I was young, but I knew there was a whole lot more to life than just football and a whole career ahead of us. Nothing was going to get between us, not even the starting quarterback job at the University of Kansas. Our friendship was going to be too strong."

——◆——

There is no doubt the hamstring thing hurt him. It was a matter of making plays, and I proved I did that good enough for the coaches to give me a chance. I have a world of respect for him because of the way he handled it. Kerry could have transferred to any number of schools who would have loved to have him as a quarterback because of his size and what he showed as a freshman. But that's just not who he is. So you gain even more respect for someone who does what he did.

And for him to turn around and catch more than 200 passes in two years, it was awesome that he could have that success because there was no one more deserving of that.

——◆——

Fine said, "The kind of cool thing about Kerry and Todd is they both possessed different skills that could have given us advantages. They both have that 'IT' factor. Todd has that as a quarterback. Kerry has it as a receiver. I think everything turned out the way it was supposed to be and meant to be. Todd had an unbelievable career. At the time it was frustrating for Kerry because I know he wanted to be a quarterback. But if you look at the course of events now, Kerry just got drafted in the fifth round as a receiver. He might not have had that high a draft position as a quarterback."

——◆——

The idea of Kerry playing receiver didn't develop until three or four games into the season. We were out there and doing well. But you always want to get your best players on the field. Coach Warinner was probably out there saying, "We are good. We're killing people, but why the hell do we have Kerry Meier, who is one of our best athletes and best assets, on the sideline? We have to find a way to get him on the field."

—◆—

Meier said, "I think it was the third week when Coach Warinner and Coach Mangino came up with the idea and approached me and asked if this was something I was interested in. I jumped all over it. Without a doubt, anybody who was going to offer me an opportunity to come in and try to help this team, that's where I want to be. I appreciated and respected their confidence in me to give me the chance to continue at a different position. I think it has turned into a blessing in disguise with where I am today."

—◆—

Of course Kerry said, "Yeah. I want to play. Whatever I can do to help. Plus, I just want to play football." So he started taking some reps. He saw limited action because we still had Derek (Fine). But he played a little bit that year and made some great catches.

He was still the backup quarterback all the way through his senior year when they finally let Kerry concentrate on being a receiver.

—◆—

Sharp said, "It's sort of funny with all that bad luck that Kerry was having and going through and everything. When Todd won the job, it was probably the best thing that ever happened to Kerry."

—◆—

The other thing I could do after they made the announcement is that I could concentrate on being the leader of the team. When you are in a competition, you are more focused on getting your reps and capitalizing on your chances. Once you become the starter, you have some other things you have to do. You have to be enthusiastic. You have to be a little more vocal. You have to show you are going to be a leader.

When you are still competing, people aren't focused on whether you can be the leader or not because they don't know you are the guy.

That's not your primary focus. Your primary focus is making your own plays. You are vying to be the leader.

Now I'm extremely confident in myself. But I got the sense that everyone felt like I had deservingly been announced as the starter. At least it felt that way to me. You never really know what someone is thinking. You might sense that someone is thinking it shouldn't be you, but they usually won't tell you that unless they are just an ass. But because I had played the year before, they knew I could go out there and make plays. They knew I was capable of turning a bad play into a good play.

If there were any doubts before, the way I showed up in my first start let everyone know I am for real, and I am here to play.

⎯⎯◆⎯⎯

Mangino, following Reesing's first start, said, "Here he was starting his first game in Division I, and you'd think he's been doing this for 10 years the way he approached the game, the way he warmed up, the way he carried himself on the sideline. Courage is a big thing, and he has it. He has this competitive spirit about him that's hard to describe. The kids feel it. The coaches feel it. He's confident and makes people around him confident."

⎯⎯◆⎯⎯

Mayes said, "I don't think there was any controversy about who won the job. A lot of the guys wanted Todd to be the quarterback and knew he was the guy — especially after his first game we knew he was the guy."

⎯⎯◆⎯⎯

The next few weeks were the same deal. I played at a high level in those first four non-conference games, which was big. I still wasn't fully understanding the defenses on every play. I wasn't always seeing the blitz when it was coming. But I was creating. I was making plays. When I didn't know, my legs bailed me out and I would run for yardage or make a throw. I was just out there reacting, just playing football.

I felt comfortable. I felt like it was my job from the announcement. But after that first game I knew, "Hey, I got this in the bag. I can do this. This is my offense. This is my team to lead. There is no doubt about that." But to come out in that first game and play like I did helped my confidence even more. After that I didn't have to worry about people saying I didn't deserve to be the quarterback or question why Kerry isn't in there or that he would have done better than that.

I didn't have to worry about any of that talk getting into my head, and I could just focus on, "Hey, I proved it. Let's go out there and do it each week." In a few of those games Kerry came in and played. I think that year he was 18 of 24 with three touchdown passes. He came in and did just as well.

THE 2007 NON-CONFERENCE GAMES:
KU 52, Central Michigan 7
KU 62, SE Louisiana 0
KU 45, Toledo 13
KU 55, Florida Intl. 3

Getting ready for the conference

In those first few games, the action definitely started to slow down week by week, and I started to settle in and get relaxed and get a feel for everyone around me. But it was a huge difference when we got to the conference because the first conference game was Kansas State.

We had won our first four games by an average of 30 to 40 points. Now we are going over to Kansas State where we hadn't won in 18 years. So there is a buzz. "Are we that good or do the people we played just suck that much?" Even after we just murder everybody running and passing and the defense is killing, there is already that talk starting. So it's kind of like, "Well, we'll see how we do against Kansas State and see if we are as good as we think we are."

> **" Are we that good or do the people we played just suck that much?"**

—◆—

Fine said, "Looking back from a couple of years when I don't have to sugar-coat my media talk any more, regardless of who played quarterback, we were going to have a special team. That year we just had a special group of guys who loved each other and played well together."

—◆—

Derek's right, we all knew we were that good. We knew how much better we were than in 2006. All the guys inside our room knew, but the coaches didn't let us think about it too much. They kept saying, "One day at a time, one week at a time, let's just keep on because we still have to get better." Coach Mangino just pounded it into our heads constantly that you have to keep sawing wood.

Everyone outside the program helped us with that because they were all saying, "KU isn't that good. They haven't played anybody."

So we get to Kansas State (KU 30, K-State 24), and we want to come out and make a statement. We want to break that streak. We want to prove that we beat the teams we murdered because we were that effing good. So first play against K-State we want to come out and make a statement. We put Aqib (Talib) in as a receiver, and we try to hit him on a post real deep. There is one of those stiff Kansas winds blowing in my face. It is my first Big 12 game starting. It is Kansas State. The place is bumping loud. I know the history.

So first play, I don't get a tight spiral. The ball flutters and it gets intercepted. So I am thinking, "Holy crap!" I think I had thrown only one pick the first four games before that. In a way it was kind of good to get that out of the way because after that I kind of settled in. As the game progressed, I got more and more comfortable. We have another terrible play where I throw a little bubble route to Dexton (Fields) that bounces off his helmet about 20 feet up in the air. Guy runs underneath it and catches it and picks me off again.

But the defining moment of that team, the first big moment when we knew we had the backbone to be a really good team, came in that game. They went down and scored to take the lead in the fourth quarter. We get the ball back and drive 70 yards, just methodical ... huge third-down conversions. We hit Dexton on a big play, a slant that goes 25 yards for the touchdown. The defense holds them, we drive down again. We should have had another touchdown that would have sealed the game on a ball that went through Derek's hands that he would die to have back. We ended up getting a field goal.

Then, you know how great teams stop people on defense at the end of the game? Aqib gets an interception off (Josh) Freeman, which is probably his fourth or fifth turnover of the game, and we seal the deal.

Our locker room was crazy. They had to have heard us over in their room because we were so loud. Coach (Clint) Bowen, who had been at Kansas all 17 years of those losses in Manhattan, he is in tears. The fact that we had won in Manhattan and did it the way we did with offense and defense ...

—◆—

Mayes said, "That was when I knew we had something special. We came out and didn't really look sharp. We hadn't won in Manhattan in I don't know how many years — it was a long time because they had dominated us for a long time. So to go down there and work through adversity. Basically that's when I personally knew we had something special. It really seemed after that that we really clicked. I like to use the term 'swag.' I think that is where we got a lot of our 'swag' from."

—◆—

Once we got that first big road win, which winning on the road is something Kansas hadn't done very well at all the first seven years, but to do that against Kansas State and to win on the road in the manner we did when we didn't play perfect but stuck it out. That was the first big win of the season, and it came down to the fourth quarter and we won it in a gritty fashion. After that, we are flying high. Our confidence is really big.

—◆—

Fine said, "That really was a big game for us. At the time Kansas State was No. 24 in the nation or something. That really set the tone for us. Coach Mangino hadn't had a really good record in conference games on the road. But we won that game against a good team on the road in a rivalry game. It was almost like the whole team was thinking, 'We can do this. If we can come here and win, we can win everywhere.' That was the attitude we took in every game."

—◆—

The next week against Baylor (KU 58, Baylor 10) was one of the screwiest games I have ever played in. There were rain delays the whole game. It was fall break so there weren't a ton of people in the stands, and it became one of those games you just want to end.

We had to go back inside twice because of lightning, and there wasn't a lot of enthusiasm. Going back and forth, you loosen up and get into the game and your adrenaline is going, then boom! You have

I took off on a 53-yard run against Colorado in 2007.

to go inside and sit for 30 minutes and then come out and warm up again. The fans aren't into it anymore. And if it isn't a close game, you really lose interest, and I know we were thinking, "Can we just get this game over with?"

We were beating them. We knew we were going to beat them, so can we just finish this game with no more rain delays?

Then we go to Colorado (KU 19, CU 14). It's another road challenge, and Boulder is always a tough place to play. This time they had just beaten Oklahoma, which was ranked No. 3 at the time.

Everyone brings up the altitude factor, which really isn't a factor at all. But the media just goes crazy with it, trying to make it into a big factor in how you play — like you are going to run a play and you will be so out of breath you can't go any more. That's so much bull. Maybe you don't want to run a marathon at a mile high, but you can play a football game and you are going to be OK. You have been training for a whole year. I think you can handle four 15-minute quarters up there.

But that game was one of our worst performances on offense. It wasn't that we played terrible, but what they were doing gave us the most problems we had all year. The style Colorado plays in the secondary is kind of unorthodox and different. At times it can hurt them because they take a lot of gambles that don't pay off. Other times it's just confusing enough you can't really get a bead on what they are doing. We weren't getting into the right plays, weren't executing well. All those things together gave us a hard time.

We weren't moving the ball. We weren't scoring like we had the past six weeks where it was just easy. It was the first real challenge for us on offense to move the ball. Because of that it became the first real challenge for our defense because we weren't going to score 45-plus points. They were going to have to get stops. The defense came up big in that game and got some huge stops.

So another road win. Once we had two road wins, and they were close games, we were just cruising.

The next week was definitely a payback game (KU 19, Texas A&M 11). I had a coach from A&M call me when I was a junior in high school, and he literally said, "Todd, you know you are not very big, not the strongest guy, not the fastest guy. So right now we have you on our B list of quarterbacks." The guy had the audacity to sit there and say that to me. I was thinking, "You might as well say there is no chance you are ever going to play here."

I remember I told Coach Mangino that once, and all that week he kept bringing it up about how I wasn't good enough to play there, kind of trying to put a little fuel onto my fire. I had a lot of friends and family coming to that game because it was the first time I had played in Texas. A lot of my buddies drove over to the game.

—◆—

Debi Reesing, whose father attended Texas A&M, said, "Todd's high school coach came. We had relatives. We bought so many extra tickets because it was in Texas. To come out at A&M and get that win, you just go, 'Wow, we are on a roll here, folks.' At that point A&M was still considered one of the southern power teams on par with Texas and Oklahoma. To roll in and beat A&M on their home field was huge, and it was just really special for all the relatives and friends and everybody who went to the game."

—◆—

It's a big game, and it's a really cool place to play with all their chants and stuff. But it isn't as loud and hard to play as you would think. Their stands are far away from the field so they are not right on top of you like Nebraska is.

It was the only game of the season when I didn't have a passing touchdown. We didn't have a whole lot of passing yards. But B-Mac (Brandon McAnderson) had a great game that day (183 yards rushing). B-Mac and the defense and the offensive line blocking for B-Mac were the reasons we won. The passing game really didn't do a whole lot for us for the second week in a row. One of the key plays for our defense came on a huge fourth-and-1 stop in the second quarter. The game was still scoreless, and they had driven to our 9.

Tight end Derek Fine (left) and linebacker James Holt — a pair of Okies — were my roommates in the 2007 season.

Their big fullback, Javorskie Lane (the J-Train), came into the game doing the little train thing with his arm like he was going to get the first down easily. And our undersized linebackers (James Holt, Mike Rivera and Joe Mortenson) just stuffed him for a 2-yard loss.

I remember James jumping up and down after that. So we squeaked out one. The thing was it was a gritty win. The defense had to make huge stops, and we won by running the ball in the fourth quarter with the offensive line creating holes and B-Mac taking over. We ran the ball 46 times that game for 227 yards. It was good to see we could win in a different way and it wasn't always going to have to be the passing game. It could be the defense and running game. So at that point we knew we had an all-around team, and we could win any way we had to. At this point there is no slowing us down. We are full steam ahead.

—◆—

Sharp said, "We just kept rolling and rolling and rolling, and it was like, 'Man we can't lose.' We just got to a point where we weren't going to lose this game, whoever we were playing. We went out with that attitude. The realization for me was after we beat Texas A&M. That was a really rough atmosphere playing. They were supposed to be great and all that. We went down there and duked it out with them and came out with a win."

—◆—

We come back home and we have Nebraska (KU 76, Nebraska 39). They are not doing too great that year and we are just steam-rolling people. So we're ready for them to come in here. We knew all week we were going to be able to move the ball. Their defense was pitiful that year. That was the year they took the black shirts away from the Nebraska defense.

So they come in. It's a beautiful day, probably the best game day of that season. There is a packed house because we're like 8-0 at this point. People are all the way up on the hill. There are not a ton of Nebraska fans like there had been in years before.

> **"We come out against Nebraska, and it was like their JV team playing our varsity."**

We come out, and it was like a JV team playing the varsity. As far as our offense playing their defense, there was nothing they could do. Every single play we called worked. When we would go out onto the field for a series, it wasn't like I hoped we could convert something and get a drive going. I was thinking, "How many plays will it take us to get a score?" I just knew it was going to happen. It was one of those games that happens once in a career. There was nothing they could do.

I don't think I got hit even once in that game. It was like a practice where I had a red jersey on. There was somebody open every time I dropped back. That was such an enjoyable game because we beat the piss out of Nebraska, who had been so arrogant and beat us for 40 years and this and that.

It was the most points ever scored against a Nebraska defense. They deserved it.

At this point in the season we kept winning, and it was getting annoying that all the national media, guys on ESPN like Mark May — who has no idea what he is talking about — are saying over and over they are going to pick us to lose each week until we lose. They have no reason behind it, they just know that at some point KU has

Kerry Meier and I had plenty to celebrate during our destruction of Nebraska.

to lose. They are not giving us credit for who we beat. They think it is all a fluke and we are beating easy teams. It doesn't matter that we are winning on the road in tough places in the Big 12 and that we are killing people. They are not going to buy into it because it is KU.

They are really thinking Oklahoma State (KU 43, Oklahoma State 28) is going to be our place to slip up. I suffered a high ankle sprain right before halftime. I got rolled up when Adrian Mayes and one of their defensive tackles fell on me. I remember it was a second down, and I still had a third-down conversion coming up next. I was just waiting there for that pain to hit you about 30 seconds after you get injured. I was trying to get this last play over with and get off the field. So on third down, I am dropping back worried that my freaking foot would fall off. I just chucked the ball away to get off the field.

I get there, and sure enough the trainer walks right up to me and he's like, "Let's wrap it up tighter." He already knew.

I get to the half, and the pain is unbelievable. Every step hurts. I get a Toradol shot. But the whole second half, I am favoring that

foot. I can't put any pressure on it. There was one play that went on for about 13 seconds where I scramble left and right. If you watch my drop on it, you can see I am clearly favoring that left foot. Same when I am moving, and it looks very unorthodox because I am trying to not use that

Todd celebrated the win over Nebraska with his mother Debi, father Steve, brother Kyle and sister Megan (l-r)

foot. That's the play where (Brent) Musburger says, "shades of Doug Flutie." But if you watch that play I can barely put any pressure on my left foot. I'm just limping around.

SCRAMBLE DRILL

When the pass-protection pocket broke down and Reesing was flushed from the pocket, the Jayhawks had a play for it. That's what made some of those scrambling completions look so easy. In this diagram, the quarterback scrambles right. The receivers from right to left are (1) running a curl, (2) a flat route, (3) another curl, and (4) a post.

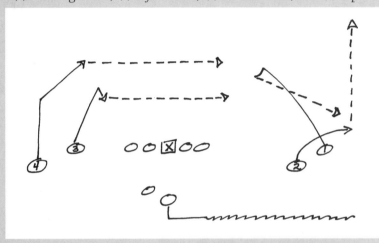

*T*he general rule when you get flushed out of the pocket is that the guy who is short goes long and the guy who is long goes short. If the outside receiver is running a curl and the inside guy is on a flat route, the guy on the flat route (2) takes off long to clear the defender out and take the defender with him. That gives the guy running the curl on the right side (1) a chance to come back to the sideline and catch the ball.

For the guys on the back side, the rule is to "haul" across to try to become a viable option; the deep guy on the other side, the same thing. Sometimes it works just as you draw it up. Sometimes you commit the cardinal sin and throw it back across your body.

A scramble presents problems — and joys — for an offensive lineman. Adrian Mayes, the starting left guard in 2007 and 2008, said, "Some of those plays where he is scrambling were the most fun I ever had being an offensive lineman. Watching him run around back there and making things happen from a blitz that we didn't pick up or a blitz we couldn't pick up. As an offensive lineman, you were really able to clean somebody's clock as Todd was running around and the defender didn't see you coming. I had a couple of those. But sometimes you would get really tired with him running around back there. There is one play against Oklahoma State where we were all running around forever back there."

We ended up having one of my best games that season. I hit Marcus Henry on an 83-yard pass play, splitting three guys — I think they all three ran into each other. I actually hit three to him that game. Aqib (Talib) had a big pick. It was really just a team win. It kind of went back and forth and we pulled it out in the fourth quarter like we had all year.

Iowa State (KU 43-28) ... the ankle feels even worse than before because it is all swollen up. I could walk, but it was all wrapped up as tight as possible. I did nothing on Sunday, Monday, Tuesday. I did a little on Wednesday and had a real light practice on Thursday.

We are trying all sorts of things to wrap it up with braces and stuff. No matter what I put on there, it still kills me. So luckily it was one of those games that we just went out and steamrolled them. It might have been my best game of the season completion-wise — I was like 21 of 26 with four touchdowns. I was just sitting there slinging it off one foot.

I am taking lazy-assed drops because I don't want to put any pressure on my foot. I am trying to avoid any chance where I would have to run or scramble. But in the first half, I think I had one incomplete pass. It was our last home game of the season, the place was sold out and rocking. People were holding up 11-0 signs. This is the game

Kerry gets the catch on the cover of *Sports Illustrated*. I was on point, for whatever reason, even though I didn't want to use one of my legs because it hurt so much to put pressure on my foot in that game.

Gun, Open right, box, lucky free, Menu 2 B-jerk

It's a mouthful to even call some of these plays, let alone run them. This is the touchdown play against Iowa State that made the cover of Sports Illustrated *in 2007.*

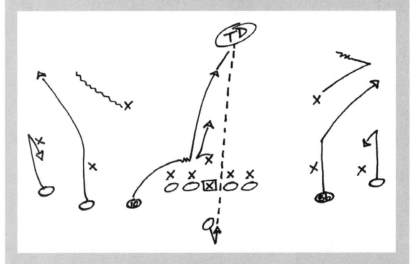

*T*his play was in our "joker package" in which Kerry is the running back, which essentially gives us five receivers. It was run from the right hash mark against Iowa State when we were in the red zone.

It's a really effective play against Tampa Cover Two, where the two safeties have deep responsibilities. Lucky free is the blocking scheme, Menu 2 is the route concept, and B-Jerk is what Kerry runs as the running back. The jerk route is named because you are trying to make the middle linebacker covering the back look like a jerk.

The basic concept has the two outside receivers running hitch routes, and the slot receivers run 10-yard corner routes. The two safeties play extremely wide to take away the corner routes, and the defense runs the middle linebacker to the middle of the field as a third guy in coverage over the middle.

The outside linebackers are going to be wider because we are spreading them out, so usually you get the four down linemen and a linebacker on the inside. So on the left side, you have three defenders covering two receivers. On the right side, you have three defenders covering two receivers. That leaves you one-on-one with Kerry working against a middle linebacker.

Kerry has the whole middle of the field to run what he wants. He can run into the middle and sit down, break left or right or take it deep — whatever he can do to get open and make the guy look like a jerk.

Their middle linebacker was a really big, stiff guy who wasn't going to be able to change directions really well. In that situation, Kerry and I both knew we were going for the big play. When we got to the line of scrimmage and saw the defense, there was kind of a head nod, like I'm going deep.

The protection was fine. The middle linebacker is cheating and starting to open up his stance like he is going to run to the middle of the field. So all I am thinking is I want to look the safeties off to make them think I might be throwing a corner route and keep the middle of the field open as long as possible.

The safeties are taught to read the quarterback's eyes. So you can't look off both sides on the same play. Because we were on the right hash mark, the safety on my left has a lot more field to cover, so he has to spread a little bit wider on our left. So I am looking at the right side of our formation because I have to sell the safety because he has the sideline and less real estate to cover.

Even though we know the ball is probably going to Kerry, the two slot receivers (Derek Fine and Dexton Fields) really have to sell their routes. The more aggressively they run their routes, it makes the safety feel threatened and the faster he will backpedal and widen. If they run a lazy route, the safety will sit there and go kill Kerry. So they are trying as hard as they can to pull those safeties toward the corner and sideline.

They sell their routes hard. Kerry runs his route and kind of hesitates for a second, which is where the middle linebacker makes a terrible mistake. Kerry just pops his hips and takes off down the middle of the field.

It's kind of a tricky throw because I have to lob it over the middle linebacker's head, who is chasing Kerry. As soon as the ball is gone, the safeties are going to be squeezing back to the middle. So you have to drop it in a bucket over his head between these two guys before he gets to the back of the end zone.

We were about as close as you could get and still run this play for him to run deep because if you are running this at the 10-yard line, you can't put any touch on the ball and he would run out of real estate.

Kerry runs an amazing route. I get rid of the ball as quick as I can after he has gotten past his guy. The ball falls in right over his shoulders just as he is getting hit. If it had been any later, the safety would have been over there and knocked it down or intercepted. The timing had to be just perfect.

Reesing to Meier

Todd Reesing and Kerry Meier made a connection that was unprecedented in KU football history. Both began their careers as quarterbacks for the Jayhawks, and when Reesing became KU's starting quarterback in 2007, Meier was the backup for the next two seasons. Yet he also became Reesing's favorite target and the most prolific receiver in KU history. The two seemed to have an innate understanding of what the other was thinking and it resulted in some of the biggest plays in KU history, from the Sports Illustrated *cover in 2007 to the game-winning catch against Missouri to uncountable catches his senior year when Meier played wide receiver full time. Meier set a KU record for receptions when he caught 97 passes in 2008, then topped that with 102 in 2009.*

I have no doubt that Kerry could have been every bit as successful as I was if things had worked out differently. Kerry was one of the best athletes we had on the team, and he would have been a really good quarterback if he had played that position his whole career. In fact, when I saw him that first spring practice I was sort of questioning whether I had made the right decision to even come to KU. He was the starting quarterback. He was an amazing athlete, and I remember thinking, "If Kerry does really well this whole season, I might not be playing ever. If he tears it up, there is not going to be a competition. Man, this could be bad. I might not ever get my chance."

There was no way it would have worked out the other way. Even though I had been a wide receiver one year in high school, when I got to college I could see the talent at wide receiver and there is no way I could have competed there.

But it was his experience as a quarterback that really helped us get on the same page, and when things broke down in the pocket he always seemed to know exactly what I was thinking as he worked to get open. And you gain even more respect for someone who did what he did and then turns around and catch nearly 200 passes in two years because there was no one more deserving of that.

—◆—

Meier said, "We see eye to eye on a whole lot of stuff. When we put in the game plan and went over certain plays, you would get a really good feel for how Todd operates and how his mind works. I really understood how Todd thought and what course of action he took on certain plays. "I was in line as the quarterback if something were to happen to Todd.

So I was in the same meetings with him every day in 2007 and 2008. Even in 2009, when I wasn't the backup quarterback, the only day I would not be in the quarterbacks meeting room was on Sunday when we reviewed the game film. Then I would sit with the receivers and break down the film with Coach (David) Beatty and the receivers. But other than that, I was in the quarterbacks room and listening to Todd throughout the week. It sure did help.

"I bought into sitting there and really absorbing everything he said throughout the week so that when Saturday came up, I knew certain little things about each play that Todd really saw and had a great understanding of how Todd played. So we had two guys who understand and come from the same point of view. When we got on the field, we really had a feel for each other and where each other was going to be."

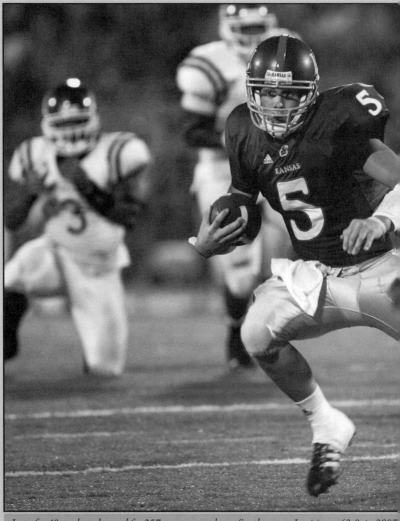

I ran for 40 yards and passed for 257 as we romped past Southeastern Louisiana, 62-0, in 2007

PHOTOS

*Todd
Reesing*

That's me at 14 years of age, ready to jack one out.

This is my Little League baseball team when I was 8 years old. I'm in the front row, third from the left.

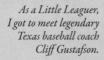

As a Little Leaguer, I got to meet legendary Texas baseball coach Cliff Gustafson.

John Cornish and I celebrate during KU's win over Iowa State in 2006.

We romped over Iowa State, 45-7, to improve our record to 11-0 in 2007.

I was one of the team captains during the 2009 season. That's me (No. 5) with Jake Sharp (No.1), Darrell Stuckey (No. 25), and Kerry Meier (No. 10).

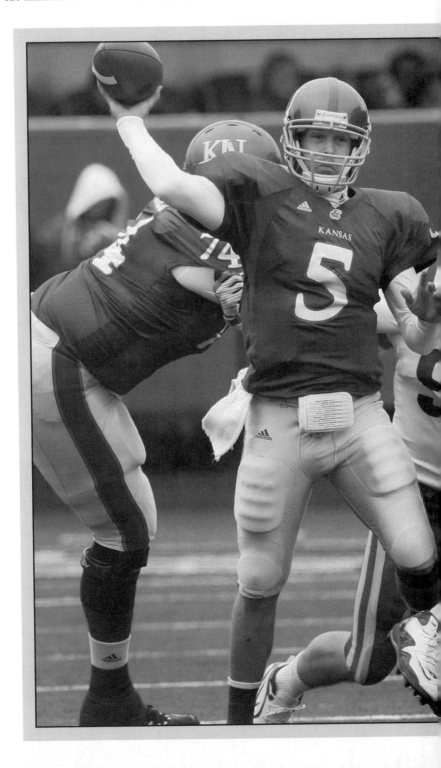

I tied a school record with 37 completions during our 41-36 win over Iowa State in 2009.

James Holt and I go crazy after our big win in the 2008 Border Showdown.

A Season of Insight (2008)

CHAPTER 7

*T*he 2008 season wasn't the overall highlight that we had in 2007, but we did accomplish something no other Kansas team ever had — going to a second straight bowl game. In our case it was the Insight Bowl, which was a great way to finish off a season.

After a rough stretch late in the year, beating Missouri in the final regular season game and then pounding on Minnesota in the sunshine of Tempe, Ariz., was an excellent way to end a year when everyone was questioning whether KU football could keep it up.

— ◆ —

Meier said he was driven through that entire off-season in hopes of reliving the 2007 season, "I had never really been on a really successful team, so I had never had a real taste or feel of being anything like 11-0 and playing in the Orange Bowl. One thing that jumps out at me is that through that whole off-season getting ready for 2008, once you have taken part in something as successful as we were in 2007, it was a driving force.

"I was driven to get back to that in 2008 and see and experience the same feeling again. Once you have that kind of success, some people take a deep breath and relax and become complacent. But the good ones continue to work and work even harder to try to get back to where they were the previous year."

The Non-Conference Games

We had lost a pretty strong senior class that played in the Orange Bowl, so I think people were kind of questioning whether 2007 was an anomaly or whether KU football really could sustain some success.

The first two games we won easily (KU 40, Florida International 15 and KU 29, Louisiana Tech 0). They weren't the prettiest of wins. They were easy. We could have been a little better. But the bottom line is that we won, and we didn't have a problem winning.

So a lot of people looked at the South Florida (South Fla. 37, KU 34) game as the first real test of what our team was going to be like. They were a team that was kind of on the rise, the same as we were. They had a lot of good talent, a couple of really good D-ends: George Selvie and Jarriett Buie. Matt Grothe was their quarterback, a guy who kind of ran around and made plays, too.

So we come out of the gates and jump them pretty good. It was John Wilson's best game of the season. We hit a pass to him, he broke a couple of tackles and got a touchdown. The defense was playing pretty well, and we go into the half with a 20-10 lead feeling pretty good — like we had a handle on things.

We come out and the third quarter was kind of the end of us. Our defense couldn't stop anything. They hit big plays. We went stagnant on offense, went two or three three-and-outs. The third quarter just killed us. So we're having to play catch-up in the fourth quarter trailing by two touchdowns. Finally we start clicking back on offense and started chucking the ball around. I was making plays with my feet and extending plays and finding some guys open. So we crawl back into the game and finally tie it with two long drives with about five minutes left in the game.

So our defense gets a stop, and we get the ball again. We are not thinking about playing it safe to try and get to overtime. We are thinking we just drove down twice on them and scored, no problem. I was thinking some big plays. My coach had the confidence in me, and he knows I want to go for it. So we come out and we are going to gun for it. We have the ball at our 40 with about 40 seconds left in the game. We have a post over the top called. Our coach thought the safety was kind of cheating. So when I look over, he points to his eyes and said take a look at this guy and take a chance on the big play.

I drop back and there was a little bit of lapse in the protection. I wasn't able to step into my throw. The ball kind of hung up, and it was a little bit under-thrown. The backside safety came in and picked it off. If we had tackled him right away, we probably still would have gotten to overtime. But he ran it back to our 27, and they could get a field goal as time ran out in the game.

It was a tough loss because we had a chance to go down and win it — or at least not lose it. It was tough on me because we had played so hard to get back into the game in the fourth quarter, making plays and running around scrambling. We had two freshmen left and right tackles going against two of the better D-ends in the country. They played really well for who they were going against. It was hot and humid — it had rained early in the game, and I was just exhausted by the end. That was really a tough loss.

So now we come home to play against Sam Houston State (KU 38, Sam Houston 14). That was a fun game. It was my 21st birthday. I had some friends come into town for that. I don't know if it was for the game or for the birthday party. But it was a game for us to get back on track, and I made one of my favorite plays of my whole career — a 60-yard pass to Briscoe that he caught in stride and ended up being the No. 1 play of the day on ESPN.

I think I found out about that when someone told me. I guess it came on the late night ESPN ... no, I wasn't in by then. We were up late that night: R.W. Logan, Pat (Sanguily), and my friends John and Melissa. Melissa is one of my best friends from back in Austin. She had come up to the game. My mother and father and brother and sister were also there. We all got rowdy. I probably didn't see the play until Sunday morning.

We had the No. 1 play of the day on ESPN during our win against Sam Houston State.

The Conference Games

So we go to Iowa State and start conference. We had put the South Florida game behind us, and we knew we were OK. What happened before the conference didn't matter now.

We come out just flat.

I mean, we are just awful.

We can't get anything going. We can't get a first down. We can't convert a third down. The defense is playing OK, but still letting Iowa State move the ball a little more than they probably should. And we find ourselves in a 20-0 hole at the half. We go into the locker room thinking, "What the hell just happened? We plastered these guys last year." We can't get it figured out.

We knew we were playing bad, and we knew we were better than them. This is where Coach Mangino was really pretty good. He knew yelling at us wasn't going to do anything good. So he came in and said, "Hey, we're OK. Just relax. It was a terrible first half. We can't play any worse. We go out there and take care of what we are supposed to do, start moving the ball on offense, we will start scoring and get a few stops on defense and we will be OK." He was very calm.

Sometimes at halftime he would try to get you fired up in a positive way and get your motor going. Very rarely did he try to chew people out at all. That just doesn't do a whole lot of good. After the game he would maybe get on someone's ass because the game is over. But he would stay positive most of the time. If you are killing someone, maybe a butt-chewing is necessary to get to guys who are not giving a good effort. But when you are behind, you have to stay positive. I think he knew when to be positive and when to get on someone. There is definitely a time for both.

So we're relaxing a little. We know we can score a lot of points really fast. We just need to get a few first downs and get things started.

So we go out there the second half, and this was kind of Jake's (Sharp) big half. We hit like a 60-something-yard touchdown on a wheel route to him out of the backfield. He later broke a long run on a shovel pass. So we start clicking on offense. It was that long touchdown pass to Jake that got us started. Sometimes that's all it takes to get the momentum swirling around, and just like that we were able to get back on track. The defense got motivated, and we were able to pull it out. (KU 35, Iowa St. 33)

That was one of the bigger comebacks in KU history, especially in Coach's (Mangino) era. It was good to have the resilience to fight back after being down like that.

So we come home for Colorado (KU 30, Colorado 14) and yet again, we didn't have a great offensive output. Same problem, we couldn't quite get a bead on what they were doing in the secondary. It was better than the year before, but not great.

The defense had a great game. Colorado's offense that year was dog-awful, and our defense was getting turnovers and getting us good field position. Not an easy game, but not a really exciting game that I can remember. We got the win and took care of business and moved on. You're 2-0 in the conference and where you want to be.

The next five weeks were rougher.

We go down to Oklahoma. They are No. 4 in the country or whatever. But we're 2-0 in the conference, and we're feeling pretty good. Our feeling was, "Why can't we go in and upset OU in Norman? What's stopping us?" We had the talent. As coach would say, "The time is right to beat OU, let's go do it." We have a great week in practice. We are enthusiastic. And we're going down there 2-0 in the conference.

If you look back on OU's season, except for their game against Texas that they lost and the game against Florida they lost in the National Championship, the only other team that gave them a run for their money was us (Oklahoma 45, KU 31). We were the only other team that made them have to think twice about it. Despite the fact they had over 600 (674) yards of offense, we had a pretty huge game ourselves (491 yards). Briscoe had about 270 (269) yards receiving against them, which is the most any single receiver ever had against the OU defense. Our offense put more yards on an OU defense in Norman than ever before.

The problem was they were just so good on offense, and they were just scoring at will. Even with us scoring here and there and having some good chances, we could never quite get within striking distance. We had a few missed opportunities in the first half in the red zone to get touchdowns that if we had capitalized, it would have made it closer. We were there at the half. We were in the game most of the way. They just had too much offensive firepower, and we couldn't get there.

We played a solid game, but we came away upset because we knew we were close. At the same time, they were a pretty dang good team that year. So we're not feeling too bad about that loss. OU is pretty good. Let's shift focus.

Now we have Texas Tech. It's a beatable team, though they are doing pretty dang good, too. We come out that game, and I'm excited to play Texas Tech. I am thinking we're going to have a shootout. Let's go out here and see if we can score more points.

The first two drives we are clicking on offense. I throw two touchdown passes, one to Kerry on a nice play-action over the top when the safety bit on it; one to Briscoe in the back of the end zone on a post route. So there are four touchdowns right in a row, and we're tied 14-14 at the end of the first quarter. I am feeling like I am in one of those grooves, hitting on my passes, seeing the field well.

Everything is working out. Then it hits the fan. Everything blows up. The second quarter we didn't have the same kind of groove. They keep scoring every time.

So we go into halftime kind of down, but we're thinking, "OK, we will battle back. Defense will get a few stops. We just need to find that groove we were in in the first quarter." Then I come back out and throw three picks in the third quarter. I think I threw two of them on back-to-back passes.

I had never been in a game where I came out and was on fire, two touchdown passes in the first quarter and feeling like it would be one of those days where you could put up a lot of points and could give them a run. Then you flash forward to the second half, and it was a completely different start. I don't know why. Before you knew it, things got out of hand and we got our asses blown out (Texas Tech 63, KU 21). That was so disappointing because of the way we started. I had never seen a transformation in one game when we were playing so well in one quarter to playing so bad the rest of the game. That was new to me.

Now we're hurting after those two weeks. But Kansas State is coming up, and any time you are playing them it gets you excited. Jake had a huge week that week. I think he had four touchdowns and rushed for 181 yards or something (KU 52, Kansas State 21). This was Ron Prince's final year at K-State, and their defense ... they were trying to do anything they could to stop us. But we could have told them the play and they wouldn't have been able to stop us.

All I know is that they came in and we are ticked off. They were in our way, and we beat the crap out of them. We ran the ball all over them, which was kind of uncharacteristic for our season. Their defense just couldn't do anything against us. We killed them.

> **"This was Ron Prince's final year at K-State, and their defense ... they were trying to do anything they could to stop us. But we could have told them the play and they wouldn't have been able to stop us."**

So we're still in the running for the North. We have Nebraska, then Texas and Missouri. If we can beat Nebraska, regardless of what happens against Texas, we should have a chance to be in the Big 12 Championship game if we beat Missouri.

So we go up to Nebraska. It's the coldest game of the season. There's a blistering wind in the stadium. You look over on the Nebraska sideline and they are wearing big ponchos, they have beanies, they have gloves on. No one on our sideline has jackets. No one is wearing gloves, no beanies for our ears. That was kind of our mentality. Coach said we are going to be some tough sonsabitches. We don't need coats or hats. It doesn't matter if it is cold or the wind is blowing. We are going to be tough.

Their place is rocking because we just pasted them the year before, and they are looking for some revenge. We come out, and the game was literally a dogfight. I keep getting blasted, even after I get a pass off that game. They were out to hit me whether it would cost them a penalty or not. They made that clear the whole game. This was Bo Pelini's first year, and they wanted to change the attitude on defense. That was probably the most beat up I had been after a game — that and the Orange Bowl.

It was probably the worst I ever felt after a game. My whole body felt bad, top to bottom. That's also the game where Ndamukong Suh messed up my shoulder. Thanks to him, my tendons still click every time I raise my shoulder. This is the game where we get a big play when I got my butt knocked back and the defensive guy couldn't stay on his own feet. I just bounced off him and we get the touchdown pass to Kerry.

We get a lead in the first half, hit some big plays. Briscoe is making some plays, so is Kerry. I am having to run around a little bit because they were having some good pressure. But we're feeling pretty good at halftime. We're tied, and we're actually leading by four with only four minutes left in the third quarter. Their defense made a couple of big plays against us because their D-line was getting pressure.

I know we had one play where John Wilson had a post route, and they completely blew the coverage on it. He was open by about 20 yards. I could have punted it to him for a touchdown because he was that open. But our guard was manhandled by Suh. He got up in my face before I could even think about throwing the ball. We were watching it on film the next day, and there was this sick feeling in my stomach. He breaks a post route and no one runs with him. He was literally at the back of the end zone with no one within 20 yards. That was tough seeing such a big play missed because we couldn't hold that block.

But we are battling. We get back within three points on a touchdown run by Jake, but then they score a couple of times when our defense doesn't get a stop (Nebraska 45, KU 35). We scored last in the game, but it's too late for a comeback. I have one long run, and I get into the end zone. I have a picture of the play, and there is just anguish on my face because it hurts to run at that point. I've got contusions on my thighs, my shoulders. Everything is hurting, my whole body.

But this is the kind of game if you are a competitor you like to play in. It was extremely competitive, and if you want to talk about a situation where you have to make plays every down, that was definitely it.

The loss to Nebraska changes our needs against Texas. We need to win now. I was extremely excited to play Texas. They were 9-1, 10-1 at the time, whatever. The whole week because my shoulder is hurting, I can't even lift it perpendicular to my body on Sunday or Monday. On Sunday I didn't do anything. On Monday and Tuesday I start hitting the rehab hard to try and work it out. On Tuesday they asked me if I could throw a football. I said, "No, I don't think I can even do the throwing motion yet, much less throw a ball."

So I stayed on the rehab day and night, rehabbing, rehabbing. I come out Wednesday, pick up a ball. They want me to throw just to see if I could. The first one I threw about 5 yards, just excruciating. I am thinking, "OK, I have to try to see if it will loosen up." So I try to force throws. It starts to loosen up a little bit. I can make a few throws. Thursday, my coaches wanted me to actually run some plays. They usually don't want to play someone who can't do anything through the week. So I battle through and do seven-on-seven. If I wasn't constantly throwing, it would stiffen up and I would have to do the whole process again.

Saturday comes, by then it is feeling a little better. I get some adrenaline going, get some heat on it and get going pretty well. Our defense plays a great game against Texas. They have a lot of stops and keep us in the game. But as good as our defense played, they pull away (Texas 35, KU 7) in the second half.

We just never get enough of it going on offense. Kerry is out that whole game. So we were without him, and they had an extremely athletic and talented defense that year with Brian Orakpo and Sergio Kindle. They had some real playmakers on that defense.

Insight Bowl (Missouri game, see Chapter 2)

After the Missouri game, we are feeling great about getting to 7-5, happy that we kind of spoiled MU's season and got to watch them get their butts kicked the next week by OU in the Big 12 Championship game, which was fun. Actually it was funny because we played OU a hell of a lot better in the regular season than they did in the championship.

So we're waiting to see where we are going to go. Everyone is pretty happy about the Insight Bowl. It's a chance to get to Phoenix, a great city, great weather. And we're playing Minnesota. They had lost five of their last six. They are in the Big Ten, and the Big Ten hasn't exactly done a lot recently.

So we're excited because we have finished our season on a positive note. We have a good bowl game. We are hearing good things for the Insight Bowl. Minnesota has a pretty basic defense. So we are thinking let's just go take care of business. We will pull off 8-5, not a bad way to finish.

———◆———

Meier said, "Even though we didn't quite live up to what we did in 2007, we found ourselves in another quality bowl game and playing in late December — which a lot of teams can't do. For us to go to back-to-back bowl games and win back-to-back bowl games really spoke highly of where we got the football program going at KU."

———◆———

We get down there, and it is a gorgeous place. They have bands for us everywhere. They have different events set up for us. The hotel is nice. Everything about it is incredible for what people would consider a lower-class bowl. But they treated us just as well as the Orange Bowl had the year before. It is a first-class experience.

Coming into the game, we had prepared well. We had a great game plan, and we knew that they couldn't score. The Big Ten is not known for scoring, and we didn't think they could stop us.

We open the game, and on the first play we're just trying to throw a little 6-yard completion to get things started. They are trying to mix it up with their defense, and their corners are backed off. So we're going to go with a little out route to Briscoe, no big deal. Well, the corner rolls up at the snap, so now I am thinking I'll go to Kerry. But he has a linebacker hugging him.

So now I am kind of scrambling around, and Briscoe just takes off when the corner glances back toward me, which is a fatal error that all DBs do. I don't even get a chance to square my shoulders to the line of scrimmage, and I kind of loft it up there before I get hit — 65 yards later . . .

Hitting that is just unbelievable. After that play, I know this was going to be a good day. How could it not be after you score on the first play of the game? You score in 12 seconds, it is going to be a good day.

They had changed their offense a little, and they actually went ahead 14-7. But they used all their best plays on the first two series. They used a halfback pass on the first series, and something else on the second. So they have already exhausted the plays they know will work, and our defense is kind of pissed off. So for the next few series, they just stuff Minnesota and our offense starts to click.

We tie the score 14-14, and then I think I had 14 straight completions in that first half — which is my best ever and a school record. Every play we are calling ... Boom! Completion. Completion. Completion. We rattle off three touchdowns in a row to take a 28-14 lead. We are just feeling it. Every play is working. Our passing game can't be stopped. Coach Warinner is just rattling off plays, and every one is working.

We come back after halftime and score again and it is 35-14. We hit the double pass: I toss it out to Kerry who hits Briscoe.

— ◆ —

Mayes said, "We knew we were going to dominate, especially from an offensive standpoint. That was my last game, and for a lot of the seniors that's definitely how we wanted to go out. The memory I have from that game is that we did have a good time down in Arizona, but we came to do what we wanted to do. That was get back-to-back bowl wins under our belt. That's another thing the University of Kansas hadn't done.

"We always wanted to do something that somebody said we couldn't do. A lot of the time we were hearing from news people saying we couldn't get it done and we were not good enough. We always wanted to prove somebody wrong and we were able to do it that day."

—◆—

Perkins said he expected the Jayhawks to be successful again. "We had so many people back, and we had a pretty good year. I don't think anyone sat here and said we were going to go 10-1 or 11-1 and be in the Orange Bowl again. We were all hoping that, of course. But deep down I think we knew that was not going to happen again. The other thing is, in 2007, we snuck up on people. We weren't doing that any more. People took us very seriously, took Todd very seriously, Kerry and all of those guys. All of a sudden, we were the real deal."

—◆—

So it was a great time. We had a great show. That field was the best grass field I have ever played on. It was unbelievable. It was a great bowl. We ended the season on a great note, had a great offensive game. So two years in a row, we're ending the season on a pretty danged good note.

I took off the next day with nine of my buddies and my parents to celebrate my 21st birthday one more time, this time in Vegas. There were about 10 of us who went down and stayed at the Palms, spent three days there, which was a lot of fun.

Senior Year (2009)

CHAPTER 8

*I*n short, my senior year sucked. We lost seven straight games, and it seemed like we were trapped in *Groundhog's Day*. The same stuff went wrong on the field every week.

Some of the football players got caught up in fights with members of the KU basketball team. I got pulled out of a game for the first time in my football career. We didn't go to a bowl game. And the only coach willing to give me a chance to play Division I football was investigated for abusive behavior and eventually got fired.

Honestly, going into the season, anything less than playing for the Big 12 Championship and going to a bowl game would not have been the season we wanted. And it wasn't like our expectations were unrealistic. With the guys we had coming back: Jake Sharp and Kerry Meier and Darrell Stuckey and Dezmon Briscoe. We were thinking if the defense can play up to the offense, the sky's the limit.

The mindset we took is to look at how we worked in 2007 before we won the Orange Bowl. Let's go back and work like that. We weren't working to play another Insight Bowl. We were working to do better than that.

But there were a lot of mistakes and unfortunate circumstances. Turnovers killed us. Some were bad luck. Some were preventable by decision making. It wasn't just one thing. And there were times we figured that there was no way on earth that the same things could continue happening week after week. Then sure enough it would happen for two more weeks.

I'm not saying we should have won every game. But we definitely shouldn't have lost seven in a row. We were much better than a 5-7 team. Everyone on our team knows that, and even if you talk to most of the coaches we played against, they would agree we were better than a 5-7 team.

But that's how we finished up. It was the first time in my whole life that something like this happened that was extremely negative in sports. And it was new for everyone around the program at Kansas since I had been there to be in this situation where we were losing all these games.

The low point for me was the Texas Tech game when I got pulled out and didn't get to finish the game. To this day, everyone still writes that I was benched my senior year at one point, which is completely absurd. I was never benched. They put Kale (Pick) in because they didn't want to risk me getting hurt. You would be hard-pressed to think you would get benched when you have 10,000 yards passing and 80 touchdowns behind your name at that point.

So to clear it up for everyone: I wasn't benched.

The whole season was upsetting. I didn't want to have my senior year end like that. I am too competitive. I want to win too badly. I wanted so many things for the rest of the guys who had put so much into it, guys like Kerry and Jake and Stuckey, who had put their hearts and souls into the program.

The investigation

I'm sure everyone wants to know what was going on with Coach Mangino and whether that affected how we finished the season. To be honest, I don't think it had any impact at all on whether we won or lost games. By the time they announced the investigation there were only two games left in the season: Texas and Missouri.

So to say that had much of an impact on other games ... I don't see it.

I had heard some buzz from some of the guys that maybe there was something going on with Coach Mangino about the way he coaches. But honestly, there was only a really small amount of talk about it.

The way I learned about the investigation is that they sent out a mass text to the football team saying there was a mandatory meeting on Monday night after the Nebraska game. That was a little unusual because Monday was normally a day off in the season. I didn't know what the meeting was about.

There were probably some guys who kind of knew what it was all about because they were the ones who had been saying stuff about Coach Mangino or their families had or whatever. But I think most of us didn't know what it was about. I was more focused on trying to figure out how we could win a game than thinking about that.

Lew Perkins came in and talked to us, and he asked that we keep what was said private. Basically, he told us there was going to be an investigation and that some of the guys would be asked to talk to the investigator, who was Lori Williams. He briefly covered the types of things that were going to be investigated that had been alleged. But they were leaving it up to the investigator, who was supposed to be unbiased and all that stuff.

He allowed questions, but no one really asked any. It was all pretty straightforward. He basically asked for everyone to keep their mouth shut because going out and telling your friends would only make it worse for us because that would generate more talk and then there would be more you had to deal with when we're trying to play Texas, the No. 2 team in the nation.

But the feeling leaving the meeting was this is obviously going to get out and obviously going to be the only focus.

—◆—

Meier said he had heard rumblings the week before.
"I kind of heard people saying stuff before the Nebraska game,
started hearing talk of something like there was going to be an
investigation and they would try to figure out what is best for KU.
But I hadn't heard anything directly. I didn't think about it very much.
What I tried to do is convey the message to the rest of my teammates that
what is most important for this team was trying to win a few games."

I snuck out the back of the meeting because before we even got to the meeting there were media members waiting around like vultures outside the football office. I knew I was going to be bombarded the next day because that was when we had our regular press conference.

—◆—

Lisa Bergeron, a business professor for whom Reesing was a TA,
said Todd was grading papers for her when he got the call.
"They took my car because they knew reporters were waiting.
They all know Todd's car, and they wait for it. The guys were like,
'No one is ever going to expect a mom-mobile.' They parked out back,
and they were able to get out of there pretty quickly."

—◆—

Was I ever right about the press conference. The entire thing was non-stop questions about Coach and questions about the investigation when it hadn't even really started yet. I kept saying: "There is not a whole lot I can tell you, I am still trying to figure this out myself."

They kept asking how it was going to affect everything. First of all, I didn't know because I had only learned about 12 hours before that there was any investigation. And I bring out the point that they are asking how it is going to affect everything, saying, "You haven't even asked me about Texas. I am going home and playing where I have been waiting to play for four years. I have tons of friends and family, who haven't seen me play before, coming to the game. I am getting to play in the stadium I dreamed of playing in all these years, and these are the freaking questions I am getting asked."

I talked to the investigator, I don't even remember when — whether it was before the Texas game or afterwards. She was basically inquiring whether I thought a line had been crossed between coaching and making things personal: "Was a guy abused or do you think he was?" They were trying to find out what we actually knew and what we perceived. The questions were more, "Do you think a line has been crossed with you?" And "Have you ever seen a line being crossed?"

> **"Do I think Coach ever crossed the line with me? Absolutely not."**

I don't know what other guys said. I didn't try to talk to other guys about what they had said. The whole focus of the investigation was for you to not talk to other people so it would just be your opinion. Obviously, guys had different opinions on where the "line" was. It is clear that some people thought a line had been crossed. That is not my opinion, but it is what other people thought.

Do I think Coach ever crossed the line with me?
Absolutely not.

I knew him better than probably most of the guys because of the amount of time I spent with the coaches. I knew him as someone who, if I didn't do things the way I was supposed to do them, I would hear about it. But at the same time, when you would go into his office he would sit there and bullshit with you and talk about your family and the things you wanted to do after football. I think of him as a guy who, if you

My roommate, Liam Kirby, and I at one of our hangouts in Lawrence, Johnny's Tavern.

called and had played for him and done the right things, and said, "Coach I need some help, can you do this?" He would do pretty much anything he could to help you.

— ◆ —

Liam Kirby, Reesing's roommate, was friends with a number of players on the football team. He said, "Mangino related to Todd because Todd was his golden ticket. But he didn't relate to some of his other players very well. Todd probably wasn't aware of everything going on because when he gets zeroed in on what the goal is (winning games), he stops picking up on some of the nuances."

— ◆ —

Bergeron said, "He really can compartmentalize things very well."

— ◆ —

Some of the things that were reported about dipping into personal lives, most of those I never heard. He brought things up to me. When I would fumble in practice, he would say things like, "I don't know how you did things at Lake Travis, but you are not going to play football that way here" or "Maybe you can be loose and careless with that ball in high school at Lake Travis, but not here." If you consider that getting personal with a reference of where you are from, then coaches are personal all the time.

The way Coach Mangino coaches is that he wants to kind of test people to see how you respond. A lot of guys rise up to the challenge when they are tested by Coach and a lot is expected of them. I remember when I was first there I got chewed out more the first half year than the next three years combined. Once I knew how they wanted things done and what was expected of me, I did it and there wasn't any problem. Some guys, I guess, don't respond to that.

The whole investigation thing sucked on a couple of levels. First off, it happened during the week of the Texas game where I was going home. Before the season I was envisioning we were going down to play Texas, maybe undefeated, maybe not. But at least with a darn good record, one ranked team playing an even higher ranked team. Maybe it would be a late-evening game on ABC. I get to play in Austin, the perfect setting.

Instead, flash forward to present day. I am riding a five-game losing streak. I am not getting asked one question about going home for the first time. And there is an investigation going on of the one coach who gave me a real chance to play with unwavering faith. I am thinking this isn't exactly how I drew it up, I guess you could say.

You could go back and forth on the way Coach handled it, should he talk about it or should he not. The way he approached it was how I would expect him to. He liked discipline. He wants things organized, wants things to run in a smooth manner. There was no talk of it. When we were in the team meeting room, we talked about how we were going to game plan to beat Texas. When we were on the field there was a little bit of undertone that everyone kind of knew what was going on and maybe was thinking, "Is this kind of weird that we haven't talked about it?"

But everyone knows. Everyone in the state of Kansas knows. It's the first time we have been on ESPN in a month, and that's the story. We go through the whole Big 12 season, and the only time we are getting any coverage, it was about this. You could sense that people were kind of thinking about it but not saying anything. But the coaches never let us get unfocused. They coached us the same way. They were still hard. They were still spirited. They knew things hadn't gone our way, but we had been playing hard and preparing hard. We just couldn't find a damn way to win.

I don't think if Coach had made an address and brought it up to the team it would have changed anything. We knew it was going on. He knew it was going on. And all the guys on the team understood the situation.

Like I said, Coach and I never had any problems. He was a constant supporter of mine during all four years at KU, from my recruitment all the way through my senior season. In fact, I asked him if he would be willing to contribute to this book, and he very kindly said yes. Here is his reminiscence of my time with the Jayhawks:

Todd was a playmaker

During the early summer of 2005, one of my assistant coaches, Tim Beck, walked into my office at Allen Fieldhouse and asked if I would be interested in looking at a video tape of a high school quarterback from central Texas. Major college football programs receive literally hundreds of unsolicited video tapes from prospects from around the country. At Kansas, we looked at every tape and made a real effort to provide an unbiased evaluation of every athlete. Once in a while, we'd find a diamond in the rough. This book is about one of those diamonds.

I popped the tape into my VCR and, after about half an hour, I sensed that this was no ordinary high school quarterback. This undersized dynamo made play after play with his arm, legs and intellect. He was a fabulous playmaker who made things happen. The only drawback was his size; he didn't look very tall. I wasn't immediately put off. After all, Bill Whittemore, our quarterback in 2002-2003, wasn't very tall either, but he was one heck of a player.

Our offensive coordinator at the time, Nick Quartaro, also evaluated the young Texan. He agreed the guy was a talented player, but expressed similar concerns about his size. I returned the video tape to Tim with a note saying, "I'd sure like to meet this kid." As fate would have it, Tim learned that the Texas quarterback and his father were planning an unofficial visit to K-State. Tim arranged for him and his father to stop by Lawrence before they returned to Texas.

Coach Mangino and I always had a positive relationship.

A couple of weeks later, the young QB and his dad arrived at our offices for an unofficial visit. I first met him in Tim Beck's office where he and his dad relaxed after the drive from K-State. When I walked into the room, this baby-faced kid stood up, extended his hand and said, "Hi, Coach Mangino, I'm Todd Reesing." Instantly, I realized my concern about his size was not unwarranted. Todd was not very tall. But he looked me in the eye with a kind of confidence that is uncommon in 18-year-olds. I spent about five minutes talking with Todd and his dad. As our conversation concluded, I realized that Todd was no ordinary kid.

While our assistant coaches took him on a tour of our complex, I went back and took another look at his high school highlight tape. During Todd's high school career he earned the Texas 4-A player of year. I was convinced he could contribute to our program in a meaningful way. I discussed my impressions with our offensive coordinator. I told Nick Quartaro that Todd was smaller than I had expected, but that would not be the deciding factor. There was something about his presence that I liked and I was going to offer him a scholarship.

I met with the Reesings in my office before they headed home to Texas. I came away thoroughly impressed with not only Todd, but with his dad, as well. I felt confident in offering him a scholarship. A few weeks later, Todd called to tell me that he was committed to playing college football at the University of Kansas. Todd had only had three Division I scholarship offers. No other BCS Conference school had considered him a big-time quarterback, but I knew he was the right fit for us.

Todd graduated from Lake Travis High School a semester early so that he could enroll at Kansas in January of 2006. His transition from high school to college football was a little bumpy that first spring. Yet, he had a certain swagger. He exuded confidence and his teammates immediately appreciated his talent, intellect and work ethic. On the other hand, his transition to college-level academics seemed to provide less of a challenge. He was immediately admitted to the university's honors program and excelled at a high academic level throughout his four years on campus.

During Todd's four years on the gridiron, he led the Jayhawks to one of their most successful runs in literally a hundred years of college football. He passed for almost 12,000 yards and threw 90 touchdown passes during his career. He led KU to back-to-back bowl wins in 2007 and 2008. With Todd under center in 2007, we posted a 12-1 record and defeated Virginia Tech in the Orange Bowl and ended the season ranked 7th in the nation. Our 2007 Orange Bowl team featured many talented players and Todd was, as we say in football, the chauffeur of our limousine.

Todd was a young man determined to prove himself, even though everyone said the odds were stacked against him. Few Division I schools thought Todd had the size to be a successful big-time quarterback. We looked beyond that at KU and it made all the difference. Todd was determined to be successful and prove the naysayers wrong. In the process, he became one of the top quarterbacks in Big XII Conference history and arguably the best quarterback ever to play at the University of Kansas.

Todd is a young man with a strong will and belief that there are no boundaries, except those you impose on yourself. That's Todd's way. I know — I was his coach.

— Mark Mangino

We want to be the hunted

A season really begins with winter conditioning when you start those grinding 6 a.m. runs and lift four days a week. We got after it. Everyone is working hard because we know the potential for our senior year. There are a lot of guys who had won two bowl games and won a lot of games. And there is strong senior leadership. So we get off to a really good start.

It's hard to say how that compared to the off-season before the Orange Bowl year because I was still pretty new to the program and wasn't even the starting quarterback. Every off-season is different, and this team had experienced winning and we knew what it took to get there.

So we are working like we expected to be one of the preseason favorites. We want to be the hunted. The first five practices of spring are a little slow to get going because some of the young guys on the line and on the defense were trying to find out where they fit in. We couldn't just come in and pick up where me and Kerry and Jake and Briscoe were and run the plays we were running the last two weeks of the season. We had to step back and start from square one and build it back up.

For me, it came down to helping those young offensive linemen get confidence. I wanted to be better than I was in 2007 and in 2008. I really want to go out and make a statement my senior year. So I am working to get fundamentally better.

Over the summer, it is good. They push us harder and make us work harder that summer than they ever had. It was a good summer, so everything is as it should have been leading up to the season.

The coaches knew they had all the pieces. They were trying to make sure that they were all in place and every edge was sharp. Briscoe had some issues in the off season. He missed spring practice and a lot of the summer just trying to get eligible. That got a lot of attention because he was the most talented guy on the offense with the highest potential draft ranking. That was a negative aspect, and he had his issues, but everybody else was moving ahead together.

Then we get to two-a-days. I am on fire. I have never had as crisp a series of practices as I did that first week. We go through the first seven practices without throwing an interception. I think I go the first

I'm making sure we're all on the same page against Texas-El Paso.

five days of seven-on-seven drills without an incompletion. The ball just isn't hitting the ground.

We aren't shooting for going eight-of-10 in seven-on-seven. If we aren't 10 of 10, it isn't good enough. If the ball isn't catchable every time I'm not happy. We are practicing at a very high level. Everything is feeling good, and we are geared up and ready to go.

The only thing I am thinking is that there is no doubt our offense is going to go out and kill it. We are going to be clicking. If the defense goes out and plays as good as they can play, we will cruise through the first four teams and get ready for Big 12 play. We are going to go out and give Texas and Texas Tech a run for their money.

Jake Sharp and I celebrate during our victory over Northern Colorado in 2009. Jake scored two touchdowns that day.

The non-conference

So we start the season. This will sound like an excuse, but those four teams we played were better than people give them credit for. Duke ended up being competitive every game they played in the ACC, even though their record didn't show it. The Duke quarterback got invited to the NFL Combine, which I didn't. Southern Miss wasn't a terrible team. They were riding like a nine-game winning streak. So we weren't playing pushovers.

And we took care of business. People were expecting that we would beat those teams 65-0 or something, and we didn't really blow anyone out. With the parity in college football now you don't have as many 60-0 blowouts like you did when Nebraska used to steamroll people in the 1990s. But people didn't like that they were close, so they started to doubt that maybe this team is not as good as we think.

You could tell that by the sort of questions we were starting to get from the media. They planted the seeds in everyone's mind. For four or five weeks, all I hear about on the offensive side of the ball is, "How come you are starting out games slow and not scoring fast in the first quarter?"

What blew my mind was that if you go back to the 2007 season, we scored on a first drive maybe once. We literally never scored in the first quarter, and in two or three of those first four games in 2009, we scored on the first drives. So I am sitting there thinking: "Are you guys watching the same game? We are not starting slow. There is nothing wrong with the offense."

After the first four games, we are in the top three or five in the nation in offense. I think we have the second-most yards gained from scrimmage, and the only question I hear is, "What's wrong with the offense?"

Obviously, it isn't perfect, and maybe we could have won by a few more points and not had as many close games. But I don't think it should have been viewed as negatively as it was. We are 4-0. We have done what we are supposed to do. We have won. Nowhere does it say you have to win by 20 for the win to be justified. That's just not the case.

HERE ARE THE SCORES OF OUR FOUR NON-CONFERENCE GAMES:
KU 49, Northern Colorado 3
KU 34, Texas-El Paso 7
KU 44, Duke 16
KU 35, Southern Mississippi 28

That adds up to 4-0 and that's all that mattered.

The conference begins

Once you get into the conference, the margin of victory doesn't matter. You have to win. It doesn't matter who you are playing or where you are playing, how good you are supposed to be or how good they are supposed to be. Anybody can win. That's been shown the last few years with all the upsets. So we go in saying, "Let's just find ways to win. We'll worry about the rest later. One week at a time."

Iowa State (KU 41, Iowa State 36) is Homecoming, and it's our best offensive performance to date. I throw for 442 yards, yet they have a chance at the end of the game to win. So now the focus shifts, and the questions are, "Well the defense isn't going to be able to hold up in the Big 12. They can't stop anybody." At least it seemed like that was the perception outside the program. Inside the program, the defense wants to step it up. They want to be stopping people and not have to win in a shootout. On offense we think we'll do it every week. If that's what it takes, OK. We'll score one more point than them.

—◆—

Meier said, "We found ourselves at 5-0 even though we didn't blow opponents out. Sometimes you show up on Saturday, it is just not your day. But we seemed to find a way to execute enough and found ourselves playing pretty decent ball throughout the first part of the season.
"Any time you can get yourself to 5-0 — there are a lot of teams that would like to find themselves at 5-0 after five weeks of the season. We were happy with where we were."

—◆—

The next week against Colorado, the defense comes out, and it's more reliable. They want to make up for what they thought wasn't a great performance. We're in Boulder, where we won a close game two years before.

That's where the wheels start to fall off my season. In the first half I have an interception when the defender cut in front of Briscoe. I probably shouldn't have thrown it to him. Briscoe isn't expecting to get the ball, so his slant route is fading a little up the field instead of sharp and crisp

Yeah, sometimes I get a little fired up.

I cut loose with everything I had on this pass against Iowa State.

down the line. And the defensive back cuts it off and makes a good play. That's my fault, and they get an easy score there.

The next series, I fumble. It was one of those deals when you have the ball in one hand and you are getting ready to throw and someone hits your arm. It's pretty damn hard to hold onto the football no matter who you are when you get your arm yanked down. Loss of ball again. They fall on it, and they get back-to-back scores. There is no reason it happened. It's not like I came out and decided I wanted to turn the ball over in the first half. But it happens. That it happened back-to-back is just freaking bad luck.

But at halftime no one is panicking. The defense looks like it is giving up points, but it was the offense that gave them up, not the defense. So they are still positive. On offense we are saying, "Hey, let's relax and go out and start moving the ball."

The second half, we are up and down the field on them. We end up taking the lead, and this is where we need a stop on defense for a chance to kind of finish off the game. They have a new quarterback, and he is scrambling all around and they have a long drive and score. So with all our seniors, we're saying, "Let's just drive down. We have done it all half. No big deal."

We drive it down, and on a third-down play we completed a touchdown pass to Kerry on the exact same route we had completed earlier in the game. The refs call an offensive pass interference on a pick play against Briscoe, which was an absolutely atrocious call by the refs. I firmly believe that to this day. He is running a slant route. He can't go in and hit the defender, but he's just running his route and stops. It's not his responsibility to get out of the way. But they call it, and we barely miss the fourth-down conversion.

—— ◆ ——

Meier said, "Honestly, it was a tough one to swallow the next day when we watched the film. But you can't fault the refs. If we had taken care of business throughout the course of the game, we never would have found ourselves in that situation. If you say something about the call, you are making up an excuse. In football there are no excuses. He assessed what he saw and threw the flag. That's the way it went. We moved forward."

—— ◆ ——

Now the defense stops them, and we have another chance. We hit a huge third-down play to keep the drive going. Briscoe makes a huge catch. Kerry makes a helluva catch and we have another chance to score. I miss Kerry with a throw that if I put it a little higher he might catch it in the corner. One to Briscoe in the end zone, he gets his hands on it with four defenders around him, and we don't get in.

It's just a terrible loss. The two first-half turnovers killed us. Getting one extra stop on defense probably would have sealed it. The refs knowing what pass interference is would have helped. The snowball started in Colorado (Colorado 34, KU 30). But if you follow Big 12 football, a lot of big upsets have happened in Boulder.

It's also where I hurt my groin — though I have no earthly idea how. Before the game it was fine. After the game it wasn't. I didn't even know I had done it until I got back in the locker room and started getting undressed.

Looking back, this is where the first allegations about Coach Mangino came out. I was completely unaware that anything happened. For all I know, most of the other guys have no idea anything happened. But apparently Coach and Arist Wright had something go on. It didn't seem like it was such a big thing that would throw us off our game. And to this day I still have not gotten the real story on what happened. All I know is what has been said and how it has been reported. I never actually heard from Arist or other guys.

And it's not like the first time he had Coach Mangino or another coach in his face yelling. He's a tough kid, a hard-working guy. He's been through ups and downs, and for all of a sudden as a fifth-year senior to think something happened that would upset him that much is still confusing. He had been with Coach Mangino, had had some butt-chewings, which everyone gets. But you never really know how someone feels about how they were treated because they may not actually voice that around everyone else. But when he was two months away from being done with football it seems strange that all of a sudden something would set him off. Maybe he told the story and someone else decided to call in. That's one of those things if you don't have all the facts, you don't really know.

The next week, we have Oklahoma, and our confidence is by no means deteriorated. We are shaken, but we aren't knocked off our horse. We know it is a speed bump. We knew we should have taken care of business and pulled that game out. But the reality is: "So that didn't happen. Let's move on. We have a lot of games left to play."

—◆—

Meier agreed, "That's exactly how we went about our business that season. The crazy part about it was that in the days following our losses, our practices continued to be spirited and there was a lot of energy and guys were working as hard or harder than they did the first five weeks."

—◆—

Oklahoma is not the powerhouse in 2009 that they are every year. We can beat them. We have a positive week of practice. Everything is going well. We have a good game plan. We come out in the game, and BOOM, same thing happens (Oklahoma 35, KU 13).

Oklahoma is probably my worst game of the season. Three picks, which I had only done one other time in my career. First play of the game, I throw a pick. We try to come out with a big play, and I take a chance and try to throw to Briscoe. I don't make a great throw, it gets caught up in the wind and he isn't able to come back and knock it down. That happens. The second one gets tipped. That one we should have checked out of the play. They are sitting on the slant routes, and I throw late to the flat. As a quarterback, the one thing you can't do is throw late to the flat. Right as I am throwing I see the cornerback, but the arm is going forward. So mid-throw, I already know I should not be throwing it. The ball flutters out and I throw the first and only ... let's see in 14 years of football ... it was the only pick-six I have thrown. I never had one in high school or middle school.

At the end of the half we have a chance on a pass to Briscoe, and if he hauls it in he walks in for a touchdown. We have our chances for big plays, we are just missing them. We are not getting any breaks. I am doing really bad. So we never really get into a groove like we did in the Colorado game in the second half. It wasn't our worst loss, but as far as how we played, it was our worst performance. We were as good as Oklahoma, and we just played terrible.

I never want to come out

Heading into the Texas Tech game, there isn't any panic. We had two bad weeks, and they were really bad. But if we go take care of Texas Tech, we're back at 2-2 in the Big 12 and going to be right in the lead where all we have to do is beat the teams after that and we are still Big 12 North champs. Knowing that, there are no hopes lost.

So we go to Tech. Everything else is behind us, OU and Colorado. We come out and we're moving the ball a little bit, not really clicking. The defense, after hearing about it in Iowa State and Colorado, they come back. They show up at Texas Tech just mad and out to prove something. They are getting sacks, causing fumbles ... the defense is really playing well. They keep us in it all throughout the game. We can't quite get anything going on offense. Afterwards, Texas Tech's defensive coordinator said it was their best game of the year.

> **"Then I get pulled. As it was perceived by 99.9 percent of the people, I was being benched."**

They had gotten shoved around the week before and had something to prove. The way things had been going for us, it was only fitting that they would play their best game against us.

So you have two defenses playing really well against two offenses that are supposed to be the best in the league, kind of a role reversal for what you would have expected. We get a shot of life when I hit Briscoe in the back of the end zone on a play that was all messed up — I almost was sacked, and was scrambling around. So we are in the fourth quarter, and we are thinking, "We've got this. Our defense is playing well. We are finally clicking on offense. We are moving the ball. We have some plays that are working for us."

Then, BOOM! Sack from the back, fumble, they get the ball and score. Try to run a quick fourth down, botched snap, they get the ball and score. It's happening again, but at a different point in the game. I am thinking there is no effing way this same series of terrible plays is happening to us again. (Texas Tech 42, KU 21)

Then I get pulled. As it was perceived by 99.9 percent of the people, I was being benched. From talking to the coaches after the fact, I guess it was more that at that point it seemed like the game was not winnable, and they just didn't want to take a chance and get me hurt. That's what I was told. Because things were spiraling out of control, there was no reason to keep me in and risk getting me hurt.

But I don't really get it. I was feeling fine. I had been playing a little banged up, but nothing that would have prompted taking me out. You never want to come out of a game. And it seemed to me like we were not out of this game. We were a couple of scores down, and it would have been a miracle comeback. But you never know. And you never want to come out of a game, especially when things are going bad. I'm thinking, "Let me finish it out. I would rather go down fighting. Let me run the two-minute twice. If I throw two more picks, so what. If everything is going bad, and I'm going to get the blame, fine. I can take it."

— ◆ —

Liam Kirby, Reesing's roommate, said it was the most bothered he had seen Reesing in their four years of friendship. "He doesn't let things get to him. In all the time I have known him, stuff doesn't seem to bother him. When I came home from work after the Texas Tech game, he was out on the roof just laying there looking up at the sky. He was exhausted and bewildered by what had happened. He had never felt that before. He had never felt what it was like leaving a game, someone not trusting him to take care of the problem."

— ◆ —

That prompts the whole next week with people questioning whether Kale (Pick) should be playing and should I be benched. I am sitting there like, "Are these people crazy? Should I be benched? They must be out of their minds." I don't think there was one person on our football team who thought there was any way it wasn't going to be me starting the next week. But any time something like that happens it spurs talk outside the program.

Now, even with all this, we still have a chance to win the Big 12 North if we beat K-State and Nebraska.

It is literally the same story at Kansas State. The defense doesn't play as well as it had the week before. The offense plays better, but not great by any means. We can't find a way to get the ball into the end zone. We are moving it pretty well, but can't get it in. K-State is running the ball pretty well. I think they rushed for more than 250 (266) yards. But in a rivalry game you know it's going to be close.

We again had back-to-back fumbles at the end of the half. They ended up getting a touchdown out of it. But in the second half we are still in it. If we get one stop on defense and we get the ball and drive down ... despite being down in the turnover margin and their rushing for more than 250 yards on us. Despite all that we are still there at the end of the game. We never get a chance to make that drive on offense. But we are right there. So there is another game that ... you know, just kind of sucked. (Kansas State 17, KU 10)

— ◆ —

K-State coach Bill Snyder, having watched Reesing play two games against the Wildcats when he was not coaching, was back on the sidelines during Reesing's senior year. "He was extremely poised, and by that I mean he could take the bad with the good. He didn't get rattled, kept his composure and, consequently, you could see his teammates really respond to his composure. Therein lies the essence of his leadership capabilities. Some quarterbacks are sensitive because they don't want the interceptions. He had enough confidence to throw the ball into what might be considered by some to be tight spots and still be effective with it."

— ◆ —

Then we have Nebraska. It's Senior Day and we come out and give it our best effort. We're playing for a bowl game against one of the best defenses in the country. We move the ball better on Nebraska than pretty much anybody had all year with the exception of Texas Tech. Our offensive line just stones their front four. Kerry has a big game. Briscoe makes some plays. We actually get back on track offensively. And we're in it in the fourth quarter. We drive 80-some yards, hit Briscoe on the touchdown and actually take the lead.

Then the defense gets a big third-down penalty — there's another thing not going our way. That allows a poor Nebraska offense to go down and score. And we don't have another 80-yard drive in us against that defense. (Nebraska 31, KU 17)

—◆—

Sharp said, "It was like a parody. We would go into the game thinking we were going to win every one of them, then something happened and 'you have got to be kidding.' Something bad would happen, and we weren't going to win the game. But every week we went in thinking, 'This is the week. This is when we break through.' We never quit. Even the last game of the year against Missouri, we were plugging away, plugging away. Looks like we have the game won, and right at the end it was just snatched away from us. You can't think of a worse way to end your career. You really can't."

—◆—

So now we're 1-5 in the conference, and here comes Texas. As I said, this was not the season I was envisioning with me going back to my home town. The investigation was announced and all the focus was on that the entire week.

I don't think it really has an effect on the game because we still prepare hard. The coaches are still coaching us the same way. We are working hard, which we have been all season. We just can't find a damn way to win because things go wrong.

This is the only game where we get flat-out beat. But investigation or not, we are probably not going to beat Texas. I am as much of a believer as anyone else that anybody can beat anyone else on a given day. But in Austin in front of 102,000 people and the difference in the talent level, we are not going to beat them.

They have freaking 700 yards (532) of offense. Our defense couldn't stop them at all. And even when our offense is moving the ball a lot, we are not going to score 50 against them. Briscoe has a big day. I am pretty on point at Texas throwing the ball. But it isn't going to matter. I showed up ready to play. I was in Austin. I wasn't going to have a bad game, and I didn't.

— ◆ —

Megan Reesing, Todd's sister who attends Texas and is a member of Kappa Kappa Gamma, said it was a fun week for her.
"We had a date function that week for the sorority. At the meeting on Sunday, one of the girls stood up and said something like, 'Hey, Meg, is there any way Todd can come down a couple of days early and be our date for this Kappa event?' Some of my friends started laughing, and I think that's when everyone started to realize, 'Like wait, who's your brother?' I guess not everyone realized that my brother was the quarterback of the team we were playing that week.
"After that, all my friends were like, 'Yeah, we will root for Todd.' But I don't think any of them were actually rooting for Kansas to win. All my friends from UT, they were all about Texas, all about Colt McCoy. So they weren't cheering for Kansas. Nobody really gave me a hard time. Maybe some of my guy friends said a couple of things, but nothing bad. It was funny.
"And that was actually the first game I had been to at Texas' stadium since it had been remodeled. I had been going to all the KU games. It was really fun having all the Kansas fans there who I had been around for so long, the families and friends of the football players I had gotten to know by sitting with them the past four years. Everyone was in my home town, and I felt like I was the host.
"The night before the game my brother Kyle got a party bus. Todd had a ton of his friends drive down from Kansas for the game. So on Friday night Kyle showed them all around Sixth Street, so all Todd's KU friends got a taste of Austin."

— ◆ —

The aftermath

Well, like we talked about before, we lost the Missouri game to end the season. We didn't go to a bowl game, and that was pretty awful. I did watch some of the games, but I wasn't watching them all like I had the two years before because there was that certain sense of, "This is going to be hard to watch because I want to be in one of those."

I still watched most of the Big 12 games because pretty much every team that was in them we had played against. So I watched them and what some of the teams they were playing did against them — like Nebraska against Arizona. Arizona had a couple of first downs the whole game, and couldn't move the ball. They were supposed to be one of the best teams in the Pac 10, and I was thinking about how we moved the ball against Nebraska compared to how they did.

In the Big 12 Championship game, you watched Texas play Nebraska. Did you see Texas move the ball very well against the Nebraska defense? Not really. So those are the things I am watching.

All the time what I am thinking about is, "Am I crazy or is it my belief that we were a whole lot better than that and stuff just spiraled out of control. Am I losing my mind?" I watched teams play the Big 12 teams we had played and realized I wasn't crazy. We just couldn't pull it together to make a bowl game.

———◆———

Kyle Reesing said, "I was frustrated for him because I know he was really frustrated for himself and the way things were going for the team and for the fans. I know everybody was expecting more than they were able to accomplish. But in the same regards, there were a lot of circumstances behind the scene that people didn't know about. He still played well. He still put up tremendous numbers. It was a tough season for everyone. I can tell you from the bottom of my heart, he did everything in his power to try and make some things happen for that team. I know that for a fact."

———◆———

*Athletic Director Lew Perkins also was disappointed for the class
that put KU football back on the map, saying, "They raised the bar
higher than anybody would ever have expected. I was very disappointed
for the University and very disappointed for those seniors. I know what a
commitment they all made to themselves and their football teammates.
It was very hard to watch when you have such high expectations. But they
never showed that it was getting them down. They came prepared to win
every game. They showed up every Saturday. They wanted to win and
they wanted to win for the right reasons."*

—◆—

I really learned a lot during that losing streak, more than I had my
entire time in college. For me it was a learning experience about life.
Things aren't always going to go your way, but it is how you respond
in those hard times that make you better. I learned a lot as far as taking
something away from sport and translating it into life.

—◆—

*Jake Sharp said, "It was obviously very, very difficult. We went
through a lot of stuff — ups and downs — that college kids don't go
through for sure, but a lot of football players never go through it. I think
everything that happened will have prepared us for anything we are going
to encounter in life. We were a little bitter with the way some people ...
well, we would definitely like to forget about it. I can tell you, never
did we think we would go on a seven-game skid. The chemistry
wasn't there. It just kind of ... the train derailed."*

—◆—

*Meier said, "Late in the season it started to get old and started to
wear. You started to get tired of it, and it really was frustrating. But I knew
that being a senior and a captain, I had to provide that positive outlook
and demeanor and carry myself in a positive manner. There were a good
bunch of guys looking up to Todd, Darrell (Stuckey), me and Jake,
and we had to continue to be positive and bring energy."*

—◆—

Debi Reesing said, "It was heartbreaking what the team went through. You have expectations going into your senior year, and obviously you want to finish strong and leave a great legacy behind. I think Todd did that. Certainly KU hadn't gone to the kind of bowl games they went to with him as quarterback. And it is certainly not the way he wanted to go out with a losing conference record. They didn't get stomped on a lot of games, but they didn't win, either."

— ◆ —

Megan Reesing said she noticed it, as well, "After those losses started to stack up, you could tell that he was definitely shaken by it. He would try not to show it, but we would know deep down he was thinking about it, going over every play of the game, what went wrong, why is it not clicking, what do we need to change. But overall I think he tried to be very positive, kept working to try to fix it."

— ◆ —

You find out who your true friends are and who is in your corner when you are going through what we did. After the Texas Tech game, I got calls from John Hadl and Danny Manning and a lot of other guys. They said to keep my head up, that I was still a leader on the team. I heard from so many guys around the University of Kansas, guys who had played sports, big-time guys, family friends.

— ◆ —

Mayes, a graduate assistant in the weight room, said, "It was disheartening to see because that group of seniors was so well-respected by all the classes who had the opportunity to play with them. They were definitely talented enough to have had a chance to be in a bowl game, but they ended up dropping seven straight.
"Todd did the same routine every week in the way he went about things and approached every game how he always had. But the outcomes were different. You could tell it really bugged him. Being in the weight room we would always see him on that Sunday right after the game, and you could tell it was eating him up on the inside."

— ◆ —

*Bergeron said, "He and I didn't talk football that much.
He had a rough year this last season, and occasionally I would say,
'How are you doing? This is not the season you expected. But how are
you?' He would acknowledge that it was rough, and it sucks, but it is what
it is. I could see the season really wearing him down. But he always tried
to keep such a good demeanor and presence about him."*

—◆—

*Kirby said, "You could tell it was weighing on him. I don't think it was
anything about his legacy at the school. It was based on him wanting to
have success for the program. He and some others had brought
KU football up to something really, really great, something special. I think
he sort of felt like he personally was letting everybody down."*

—◆—

I had so many people who genuinely cared and supported us.

It really came into focus before the Missouri game when Coach (Don) Fambrough organized his rally. We came up from practice, and there were hundreds of KU fans standing out there in the cold cheering for us as we walked into the locker room. That, for me, was one of the coolest things.

Things had gone really bad in the season. It is easy for a fan at that point to throw you under the bus and say, "These guys were jokes. They didn't care. They didn't want to win."

Those people have no idea what they are taking about. So you could be them or you could be like these fans who are going to come out and say, "We know these kids have been trying and fighting hard and things didn't go their way. But let's go out and support them." Seeing that was reinvigorating. It was really cool to see there were fans willing to come out in the cold and show support. As a senior with my career winding down, that meant a lot.

A Year of Football

9

I know that some people know how much time football takes. But I don't know how many understand exactly how you have to juggle the time commitment to be a student playing on a college athletic team — in my case a football player. I know people say, "Yeah, they have to go to school and do all this, but they are getting a free education and getting to play football, so how hard can it be?"

So I'd like to take you through a typical game week in the fall, then give you a glimpse of what it's like the rest of the year. Don't get me wrong. I wouldn't trade what I did for what any other student does.

Monday

Mondays were our day off. That's something Coach Mangino started doing a couple of years into his tenure. Instead of taking Sunday off and practicing Monday, he found it better that we come in on Sundays, watch the films and get the last game out of our heads as quickly as possible.

If you were banged up or needed treatment, then you needed to come in on Monday to see the trainer. I usually went in to watch video of our next opponent on my own. I'd go by and usually drop into the coaches offices, sit down with them and see what they were thinking about for the next opponent. They would tell me ideas they had for new plays for the next day and what we would be putting in that week. They would tell me what they thought were the best cut-ups of opponents' video to watch, and then I would watch them on my own and be on my way.

Tuesday

This was a killer day. We would lift weights in the morning: 7:30 or 8 o'clock. The younger guys would have to go in at 6. But the guys who were playing and the older guys would get the later time. Then you have class for a couple of hours.

Tuesday is always press-conference day, so I would come over right after class at 12:15 and talk to the media and do any phone interviews they requested. I would go straight from there to get dressed and taped for practice and maybe try to watch some extra film before we would meet with our coaches.

The meetings would start at 2 p.m. You had to be dressed and ready for practice by then. On Tuesdays they would hand out the scouting report where one coach would give an overview of the team we were going to play with key talking points they would emphasize. Then we would break up and go over our offensive scouting report with our coaches ... do all the stuff on the white board, new plays, new concepts, watch film of how those plays might work. Then we would practice. Practice would go up until about 6:30p.m. or so.

So you would meet for an hour and a half, practice for a few hours. Then, if you were hurt, you had to get treatment. After you shower up, it's after 7 o'clock and you head over to the dining hall to eat. So you are home 7:30-8 p.m.

At that point — if you feel like it — you do your homework. That was the hard part. On a Tuesday, when I got home all I wanted to do was sit down and rest. So on Tuesday my schedule would usually start 7:30-8 o'clock in the morning, and I wouldn't get home that night until 7:30-8 p.m.

Wednesday

You go to class in the morning, and you had to be ready for position meetings that started at 2 p.m. So I would get there about an hour before the meetings, get dressed and try to watch a little extra film. Then you would meet with your position coaches for about an hour and a half. Practice was the same thing as Tuesday and you would finish up around 6:15-6:30 and then go to dinner. Compared to Tuesday, it was a light day.

Thursday

Pretty much the same as Tuesday, lifting in the morning at 7:30-8, class, then practice. Practice would be a little bit shorter on Thursdays because we were getting closer to game day. But it wasn't a lot shorter. The only difference for me on Thursdays from Tuesdays is that we didn't have the interview sessions with the media.

Friday

No workouts in the morning, just class. If it was an away game, we would probably come in around lunchtime. Then we would have meetings, and go through a walk-through practice where we would review what we were going to do in the game.

Every Friday we had a test. Each position had a series of questions, and you had to draw out what your assignment was, what the play was and how you would execute it against the team we were playing. Each different position had a different test. The quarterbacks would have a series of questions about the kind of coverages we would see, what percentage of the time did they blitz, what their coverage percentage was, who their best players were, what our plays were if they lined up in a certain way. Those were all written answers.

Then you would have two pages of 8-10 plays per page. You would have to draw in the concept of the play you were running. Then you would draw what to do if the coverage was different or if they were blitzing. If there was something you were supposed to look for to determine the coverage or a blitz, you had to write that out.

Even though the receivers have to be on the same page as the quarterback, they had a different test because they don't need to worry much about how we are going to pick up the blitz. They are just looking at coverages. If I make a check to a run play, that doesn't make much difference to them. And I didn't give a crap about the angle they have to run to try and get a block. All I care about is that they got there.

So they probably had to draw in their routes on a lot of plays similar to our tests. But they are not looking at what I am looking at, so it's a different test.

We would travel after the walk-through. When you got to the hotel, you'd have dinner, relax in our rooms for a while. If your parents were at the game, you could spend a little time with them. There would be one last team meeting at the end of the night and then off to bed. We usually tried to time our arrival for the same time of day no matter where we traveled so that the routine was very similar.

If we were playing at home, after the walk-through we would have a team meal — there was always a big pre-game meal on Friday night. Then we would stay at the facility and watch a movie. After the movie, Coach Mangino would talk for about 15 minutes or so. We would get out of there about 9:30 to go home and go to bed before the game. We always stayed at our own places the night before a home game.

Game day

The routine was a little different if it was a morning game or an afternoon or evening game. You always had the pre-game meal. If it was a morning game, you got eggs, hash browns, bacon, fruit — all the breakfast type stuff. If it was a day or evening game it was spaghetti, chicken, baked potato, corn. It was always the same.

For a morning game you would eat and have a little quick team meeting. Each coach would ask their guys one or two questions about the upcoming game, their assignments, whatever. Then we would watch a motivational video — which was a highlight video from the game before. That would usually get you really amped up. Then we would start getting dressed about an hour before the warm-ups started.

We were always required to wear a collared shirt and slacks to the game. When I lived in the house just a block from the stadium during my sophomore and junior year, I just walked to the game because I was a block away. So I would walk to the game in my suit with everyone tailgating and walk home afterwards. For afternoon games we would usually have my dad drive us so we didn't get stopped and delayed while we were walking through the tailgaters where it was really crowded with a lot of drunk people. But for the morning games we would be heading over there early enough that not many people had arrived yet.

If you were playing a night game, you'd usually watch some of the early games on TV. I really didn't like playing the late games. But as you watched, you'd see some things in some of those games that would remind you of things you were going to try and do in your game.

The games were the most fun part of the week.

Then afterward, you had the rest of the day off.

There really weren't any difficult places to get into on the road because you usually had a police escort going to the games. They had it mapped out and got us there pretty efficiently. Since we were there pretty early, there were never a ton of people around when you got there.

At Arrowhead both teams arrived at the same point, so you had both sets of fans. That was really the worst place when you were walking off the bus because people were shouting obscenities at you that you would never say to your grandmother. But most places it wasn't like that.

So the Missouri games at Arrowhead and Kansas State were the only places where there was much yelling. I guess they do wait there to heckle you when you get off the bus. They are staying stuff that has nothing to do with football. They are just trying to cut you down personally and act like jackasses.

Sunday

If you were banged up or needed treatment or ice, you would come in around 11-11:30. We lifted weights on Sundays. There were two times: one at 12:30 and one at 1:15. We would get in a workout, just calisthenics and loosening up to try and break down the lactic acid built up from the games. The workout was really more of an extended warm-up, and the lifting wasn't all that intense.

Then Coach would have his remarks about the game, talk about the game, talk about where we stand in the season. Then they would hand out the player of the game stuff for the offense, defense and special teams. And the whole team would watch all the plays on special teams. Whoever coached that unit would talk about it.

After that we would break up into offense and defense groups. We always had offensive goals and stats we were trying to accomplish, and the offensive coordinator would break that down to see whether we had met our marks. Then we would break up by position and watch the whole film. Once we finished watching the film, we were free for that day.

I think most fans understand the game-week part of our year because for them the emphasis is on the fall when they can go to the games and tailgate, breaking out their grills for burgers, brats and parties. Maybe a little of that for the spring game as well. But the season for us really begins at the start of the second semester, long before anyone pulls out their grills for brats, burgers or beers.

Off-season conditioning

The actual season is the fun part for players. That's when the fans are around cheering and you get to go and play games. What the fans never see are the 6 a.m. runs in February and March when normal students are sleeping off last night's session at The Hawk or The Wheel. That's when the foundation is laid for whatever success or failure you have later in the year.

We go into the off-season program as soon as we get back to start the second semester. It's pretty standard for the first eight weeks. We lift and run Monday, Tuesday, Thursday and Friday. In addition to the lifting and running, we would have what we called our team station days two days each week.

All the coaches are there for those, and we're split into about eight different groups we called teams. Each "team" was made up of a mixture of players and positions. There are eight different agility stations, and you go through nonstop agility drills. The whistle blows, do this. Blow it again, do that. At the end of the session, we would do conditioning and run.

Those two days of stations were the hard ones. The coaches were there, yelling and kicking our butts. It's only about an hour, an hour-fifteen. That's when you begin to develop the mental toughness that will carry you through the rest of the year. The other two morning sessions we would do what we called "speed school." That's where you work on running form, explosive movements, plyometrics, stuff like that.

The conditioning aspect of it always happened at 6 a.m. Then, depending on your class schedules, there were about three different times of the day that you could go lift. The strength coaches would put you in the lifting session that fit your class schedule. We would lift for about an hour. They can only require eight hours of work each week in the off season. So it was four hours of running and four hours of lifting.

There are whole sets of beliefs in what is the best strength and conditioning system. Every coach has a different idea. But we were doing a different group of core muscles each day. They worked the guys based on what their level of conditioning was. The young guys were level one, the oldest guys were in level three. For some guys the weightlifting sessions were something they hadn't really done in high school. But they are building you up so that eventually you can do testing at the end of the semester. So they start you with lower weights and high reps and work your way through lower reps with higher weights.

On Monday and Wednesday afternoons, we would do seven-on-seven with everyone except the linemen. The coaches weren't allowed to be around for that, and they couldn't require you to do it. So that was always on the players. But even though they couldn't require you to be there, there was an expectation that you would be there.

The seven-on-seven drills were our activities run by the players. Usually, I was calling the plays, especially if some of the younger guys weren't really up on the offense. So we would do that twice a week, also. Usually, the quarterbacks are also meeting with the coaches. They can't require that either, but the quarterbacks are almost always in extra meetings with the offensive coordinator.

Then the weekends were free. There is a whole lot more free time during the spring than there is in the football season.

If you have gone to a bowl game, you have less time off during the holidays. When we came back from the Orange Bowl, we only had 10, 12 days off because the game was so late. You get back, and Boom! Start over. You have a new goal, working for the next season.

You're back into it, working to get bigger, faster, stronger.

Spring Practice

The general schedule is that you do Monday-Wednesday-Friday and Saturday practices. We do that for 15 practices. So you have four practices a week and probably the Friday before the spring game you have off so that it ends up just being 15 practices.

The practices in spring are pretty much the same type practices and schedule that you do in the season. You come in at 2 p.m. for the start of meetings. But since you aren't going on Tuesday or Thursday, you could have classes later in the afternoon. The difference is that every practice in the spring is like a Tuesday practice in the fall — long, grueling, full pads and full contact for part of the practice.

The Saturday practice would usually be a scrimmage.

With Coach Mangino, we would have our first week of practice, then get spring break and come back to have our last three weeks. When Coach Gill came in with his staff, they waited until after spring break to have their start. So they are going a full month straight.

We always had the week of spring break off. But I remember my first year I had a trip planned to go with some friends somewhere.

I was supposed to leave Saturday morning. When I heard we were practicing Saturday morning, I was like, "OK, Why? I thought you said we were done when spring break started." Well, of course the answer was, "Yes, you're off ... right after you practice one last time on Saturday."

During spring practice we would still lift three days a week. Our conditioning was done during practice. If we practiced hard we wouldn't have to run after practice. But if Coach wasn't happy with the way we practiced or with the effort, then you were going to do some extra running.

After spring practice, you have about a month left before the end of the school year. So you would usually be lifting four days a week and running maybe two. But this was the time when you would start to lower the repetitions and increase the weights as you got ready to do your tests.

So you have a month to get ready for the squat, bench press, 40s. It's a lot less intense than the winter conditioning program, and it was time to recover from spring ball and get ready for your finals in classes.

After school would end, we would have two weeks off for summer break. Then we would come back at the beginning of June when summer school starts, and you would have another eight weeks of summer program.

Summer program

Same thing. Two hours every day, Monday-Tuesday-Thursday-Friday. There is no involvement with the football coaches. They only have spring ball and the season. In the winter they can come out when we are doing our stations twice a week for that one hour. But I think all coaching staffs are different about that. The new staff at KU didn't do that. And there are probably some schools where the coaches never come out. Coach wanted his assistants to see their guys working.

The summer is almost the exact same schedule as the off-season program. We would run at 6 a.m. on Monday and Friday, just like in the off season. The difference was that during the summer they were trying to get you acclimated to the heat you'd have during two-a-days, so Tuesday and Thursday we ran in the afternoon. A lot of times we would wear weighted vests to simulate having shoulder pads on. We ran a lot of stadium stairs because at the start of two-a-days, you have a conditioning test — and you don't want to fail it.

We would do more position-type work on Tuesday and Thursday in the afternoons — cone drills, working on things you would actually use in a game. The weight lifting was still the same as you did all through the winter.

And we're still doing seven-on-seven on Mondays and Wednesdays just like we did. That would take us up to the end of July, end of summer school. So you would have an hour of running and two hours of class in the morning, and maybe a lift after that. You are still getting most of the afternoon off.

For the most part summer is pretty relaxing where you are kind of trying to recuperate from spring ball and get ready for the season. They can't make the workouts mandatory during the summer, but everyone is there. The way they saw it, if you weren't there for the voluntary workouts, you weren't going to be committed to the team. They couldn't punish you for not being there, but their attitude was, "Maybe we just won't play you."

So it was really kind of the players' job to make sure everyone was there. Because the coaches couldn't punish anyone for missing workouts, the players did. If you missed, the seniors would require you to do certain things. Now, obviously, if someone didn't want to do their punishment, we couldn't make them. But if they didn't do the punishment, they would hear about it from everyone on the team. And the coaches would hear about it from the other players.

Team building

A lot of the team building happened over the off-season. We had team activities all spring long, some non-football related competition things. In the whole off-season they had those eight groups that were teams. Every group had a team leader. We would do a point system. If a guy misses class, he loses points. If he misses tutoring, he loses points, if he missed a workout, he lost points. Community service got you points. Perfect attendance for workouts, you got points.

The points were recorded each week. At the end of it, if your team is at the bottom four or six, you have extra running and stuff to do while the other teams get to sleep in. That's the kind of stuff we did for team-building exercises.

During the off-season, we also had team meetings every week that we called "Character First." It was stuff that involved being a good teammate, being good in the community, how to act around women, how to act around people and generally just how to be a better person. That was something Coach Mangino wanted to make sure everyone was exposed to in his program.

Two-a-days

Two-a-days are a grind. I guess the first thing you should know is that you don't always practice twice each day. I think you can do only like 30 practices before your first game. We would probably do two practices a day only four, five, six times.

But you're staying in Naismith Hall for a couple of weeks. You are getting up at 7 a.m. and getting done at 9 o'clock at night or later every day. Almost every day we practiced in the morning and tried to beat the heat. Those few afternoon practices were to help you get used to the heat.

The hardest thing about two-a-days is the repetition. You start from ground zero. So by the time I am a senior, I am learning a play I have been taught eight times. You learn it every spring. You learn it every season. So by your senior year, you have installed these plays seven times. But because there are new guys every year, you have to start from square one.

Every day you have a set of formations you put in, a set of plays, a set of motions. You know what is coming up, and you are supposed to learn it the night before. That way you get an idea for it. But if you already know all of it, when you get in those 90-minute meetings and the coach is up there talking and drawing on the white board, it gets really hard to stay awake.

They could be doing a play where it is basic slants or something. For the young guys, they

> **66 The coach will ask you a question out of nowhere to catch you off guard when you have started to snooze off a little bit. They need to get a pack of Red Bulls in the fridge or something. 99**

don't understand what they are reading, and the drawings help them know how to run the routes correctly and read them correctly. So they need to know that stuff. But if you have played a few years it is extremely basic. I mean, you always talk through it more and study it more. But it gets tough on Day 10, and you are sitting there and the only thing you want to do is close your eyes for 10 seconds. Then the coach will ask you a question out of nowhere to catch you off guard when you have started to snooze off a little bit.

I'm telling you. They need to get a pack of Red Bulls in the fridge or something.

Practicing was the easy part of two-a-days. On some really hot day your legs are going to start to feel it, especially if you are a linebacker, defensive back or receiver who is running a lot. But the practice was the fastest three hours of the day for me. It moves along. You are having fun. You are competing, You know the season is right around the corner.

I enjoyed being out there in practice. I had a good time. It was coming back and sitting in the next 2 1/2 hours of meetings when all I wanted to do was close my eyes for 10 minutes that it was hard.

Once you get out of two-a-days, you get to move back and sleep in your own bed. We are still going on that long-day schedule. But getting out of the dorm and sleeping in your own bed, it is like you literally haven't been home in a year. Sleeping on those cots in Naismith compared to getting back in your own bed ... that's heaven to get in your own bed.

And they have taken your car keys away for two weeks. Just to be able to drive three blocks away to your own house and sleeping in your own bed is like you are escaping. Once you get through that grind of two-a-days, you get to that first game and you're like, "It's finally here." It's only been like 20 days, but 20 days in the off-season are the longest days of the year. You cannot wait to play. You are sick of each other.

You are like, "Can we just start school and hopefully some girls will show back up on campus so I can get away from all these big guys?"

Academics

The normal class load for a student was 15 hours, but most football players never took more than 12 hours in the fall. Then they would take 15 in the spring, and maybe six in the summer so they could take 12 in the fall. But you were there all summer, so there was no reason not to take classes.

Personally, I never took more than 13 hours in the fall. And actually I never even once took 15 hours in a semester. But I came in with a lot of hours. I was there a semester early. I did probably six hours in summer school. So I never had to take a 15-hour semester. I never had more than four classes. Most people usually don't get that lucky.

You had to schedule classes so they were always in the morning. Depending on what your schedule was like, you would have maybe two to three hours in classes on a Monday. But everything had to be done before noon so you would have time to get some lunch and be ready for meetings by 2:00 in the afternoon every day.

And most guys had eight hours of tutoring in a week. So during the season, when practice would get over at 6:15-6:30, then they would eat and be in tutoring from 7 to 9 or 10, and maybe during the day in free time before lunch hour.

I was never forced to have tutoring. My grades were good enough (3.64 GPA) that I chose not to have it, and I never needed it. But a lot of guys have to have it to keep their GPAs up. I only had tutoring for one class the whole time I was there. It was always offered, and you could choose it. And your advisors the first two years would always suggest it and say, "Why wouldn't you take advantage of it?" But for me, I knew I was going to go to class. I knew I would like it, and I could get my grades without having it.

> **❝I was never forced to have tutoring. My grades were good enough (3.64 GPA) that I chose not to have it, and I never needed it.❞**

— ◆ —

Reesing was a TA (Teaching Assistant) for finance professor Lisa Bergeron, who said, "He was one of the best TAs I ever had, and he was busier than most of the TAs I had. Some of them tend to push stuff off, but he always got his stuff done way before anybody else. I think people who are busier tend to get their assignments done more quickly. The TAs would come to class, they grade homework, they hold office hours when they meet with students and explain stuff. And they do any projects I have for them. But mainly grading and office hours are a big part of it."

— ◆ —

I didn't want to give up more free time to have to do that. I was like, "I'll study, but let it be of my own accord." Most guys are required to have tutoring when they first get there, then if they make good grades and show they can do it, they will make it optional afterwards.

During the season there are just times that you could only study so much, and you have to rest. Especially as you get later in the week, it was really important for me. On Wednesday, Thursday, and Friday of game week I would probably average 9 hours of sleep each night. I wanted to get a whole lot of sleep to really rest up. You never really want to sacrifice your sleep and rest for schoolwork ... not because you didn't want to study or didn't want good grades. But you physically couldn't do it. You couldn't stay up late to study and still get the rest you needed.

And especially like on a Tuesday, which is a really long day. An hour will just fly by when you are trying to unwind from the day and ease your mind. Before you know it, it is 9 or 10 o'clock, and you are like, "I have a test tomorrow, and I haven't studied." So you have to decide whether to study late at night or get up early and study the next morning. Studying at night when you are really tired is not an easy thing to do. So it is definitely a chore in the fall balancing your time.

My GPA was always better in the spring semester because of that.

Injuries

Most guys don't want teammates who are always in the training room with some sort of injury because by the middle of the season no one feels great. So if it is something minor or just soreness, a lot of guys won't say anything because they don't want to make excuses. They'll go in and ice down and do extra stretching and whatever they can besides going to the trainer and saying, "I don't feel good" or "this hurts."

But if you injure yourself, you have to tell the trainer because he will give you the best rehab and treatment to get you ready to play. If the coach sees you favoring something, he will ask you about it. If you say something is hurting, the first thing he asks is if you have seen the trainer. So a lot of times it is best to at least tell the trainer, "Hey, this is hurting, but I am fine."

I would say it's usually about halfway through the season when you really start to feel it. I'm not talking about an injury that keeps you off the field entirely. I mean the kind of hurt that football players just suck it up and play with. The first four weeks, the non-conference games, that first month is a breeze. I used to come out on Sundays after the first four games, and I was just flying around. My body felt great. My legs were fresh. I was out there sprinting when we ran. When we did our conditioning, I was just killing it.

But each week after that you start to lose that bounce in your step. You start to feel more sore after the games. If you have bumps and bruises, that's when it starts to pile up because you never get a chance to heal. If you get an injury and it's something you can play with, you don't ever get to rest it. The coaches always sort of felt like, "If you don't practice, why should we let you play?" So you are practicing all week with these injuries because you know you have to practice to play.

I have been really lucky during my football career. I never missed a single minute of football because of an injury from middle school on. I did get some injuries that kept me out of practice, but I always knew I would be ready for the next game.

That's where your work ethic pays off. If you are an older player, or a guy who has played and earned his spot, sometimes you would get a few days in practice when you wouldn't have to go full speed and you might get a few plays off here and there.

Sophomore year

In my sophomore year, I rolled my ankle on Saturday against Oklahoma State. If you have a high ankle sprain on Saturday, it usually doesn't blow up until Sunday. So you are walking gingerly on Monday and Tuesday.

There was clearly no way I could practice, but at the same time, there was no way in hell I was not going to play the following week. So I lived in the training room the week after I hurt it. I would be in there an hour-plus in the morning, an hour-plus before practice and an hour-plus after practice. Your whole damn day is spent at the football facility trying to get ready for the next game.

I had to ice. I had to do the rehab stuff with my ankle — stim (stimulation) therapy, whatever. I got in the underwater treadmill to run under water to loosen it up but not have that pressure from pounding it on the ground.

With me, it hurt really bad at the beginning of the week. That Sunday, Monday and Tuesday, it was just letting it recover from that game. Usually I would get in there and do some practice stuff on Wednesday or Thursday. Then you taper back on Friday. Get to Saturday and wrap that bitch tight as hell, get a Toradol* shot and go out there and see what happens.

Junior year

Same thing happened my junior year when I banged my shoulder up, compliments of Ndamukong Suh. It was a big bruise on my deltoid muscle where everything sort of connects up in your shoulder.

I played the whole game, but I was really beat up afterwards. When I woke up on Sunday and rolled over on my shoulder, it was like "Holy shit!" I go in to the training room, and I can't bring my arm up to shoulder level. So there was no way I can throw a football. There is not a whole lot a quarterback can do if he can't throw.

So I went out and stood at practice, taking all the mental reps. We didn't miss practice because of the injury because you can still talk through stuff. When I wasn't practicing that week, I stood next to Coach (Ed) Warriner and took a mental rep. At that point in the season, not throwing the pass didn't matter as much as long as I knew what I was doing.

The first day I tried to throw a ball was on Wednesday. I threw it about 5 yards, and it felt like my arm was going to fall off. It was terrible. I came back on Thursday and they were kind of like, "Well, we need to see you throw the football if you are going to play."

So I was like, "Screw it!" I just sucked it up and kept throwing 5 yards, then 10 yards. It was so painful. But once I threw enough, I actually started to loosen up so I could throw it 20 yards, then 25. As soon as I stopped and waited five minutes, I had to go through the process all over again.

The game that week was against Texas at home in my junior year. Once I got into the thick of the game, it was easier to keep loose. I had put the heating gel on it to keep it loose. We had heating pads I could put on there if I needed. But once it got loosened up, and once the adrenaline was going, it didn't seem to matter at that point.

Senior year

I hurt my groin in the Colorado game, and the thing was it wasn't one specific play. I didn't even know I had done it until I got back in the locker room and I started getting undressed. Then it was like "Holy shit! This hurts." But the whole time during the game I had no idea. I am only assuming it was injured during the game because before the game it was fine and after the game it wasn't.

I took a cortisone shot after the game, but I don't think it did a lot. It sure didn't make it quit hurting. So Sunday and Monday I can barely move. On Tuesday I could practice, but if we were running like a rollout pass I was only about 50 percent. That was about as fast as I could bear to go. Basically anything I did would hurt.

It became a cycle for the rest of the season. I would feel terrible on Sunday and Monday. Tuesday and Wednesday it would feel better. Thursday and Friday it would feel almost OK. On Saturday, I would take a Toradol shot, the adrenaline would kick in and it was OK. I even led the team in rushing a few of those games. So it never affected me during the game. But the other six days of the week, man, three of those sucked.

It was one of those things that wasn't getting worse, and I continued to practice. Obviously, if you are healthy and can go full speed it is always going to be better than having to practice hurt. But during the week, practice is more about understanding the concept and knowing what their defense is doing and what you are looking for. We are not putting in a lot of new stuff, so these are plays I have been running for three years. Because I can't do a rollout full speed doesn't mean I don't know what I am doing.

Some people think we get shots to dull the pain so that we can play in a game. I have never seen anyone get an injection of cortisone or anything like Novocain on game day. If they have, I have never heard of that. I don't think they really do that kind of stuff any more. When you do that, you risk getting hurt a lot more because you can't feel anything in there.

The only shots I ever took were Toradol shots on the day of the game. It's used by a lot of NFL and college teams.

* Toradol, also known as ketorolac, is a painkiller and anti-inflammatory "like Advil or Aleve, maybe a little bit stronger and in an injectable form," according to Dr. David Geier, sports medicine director at the Medical University of South Carolina. Toradol is used commonly in professional sports, including football, hockey and soccer. Toradol/ketorolac shots are intramuscular, usually given in the buttocks or upper arm.

*Away
from
the
Field* **10** CHAPTER

*Todd Reesing is sitting at a booth near the front door of
Quinton's Bar and Grill in Lawrence, Kansas. In mid-sentence,
he is interrupted by a man walking out the door after eating lunch.
"Hey!" the man says. "I just want to thank you for the
last three years. I am a KU grad, and it was great watching you
play for the last three years. You made it fun watching the
Jayhawks again, and I wanted to thank you."*

————— ◆ —————

I've found that happens all over the place. Obviously, it happens a lot more in Lawrence, and a lot more during the football season when we are doing well. That's when you are in the news more, and you are in the paper, and your face is around in front of the public a lot more.

But I was with my brother in New York a few weeks ago, just at dinner in a little bar watching a game and having a drink. Someone came up to me and said, "Hey, I went to KU, I'm a big fan." In the middle of Manhattan that happens. And I was in Austin, where my parents are, and was out with a couple of friends. A girl just walked up to me and said: "Rock Chalk." I was like, "Oh, hi. How you doing?"

One thing that is truly cool is that I have found the KU alumni are extremely strong. Everywhere I have gone there is a strong alumni presence. There are KU people all over the place. When I was with (former KU linebacker) James Holt in San Diego, down in Mission Beach they have a KU bar. There is a Jayhawk flag hanging outside and Jayhawk memorabilia all through it. They have T-shirts with a Jayhawk on the back and Mission Beach, California, underneath it.

Everywhere I go I seem to run into people who are KU fans who have watched and stuff. Most of the time they just want to say hi and that they watched the game and that's it. Sometimes they might know someone I know or have a story and we will end up talking for a while.

When I am out in Lawrence there are more people who come up to me. If you're with friends or something, you don't want to get stuck in a long conversation. I would try to be as courteous as possible because I am never going to turn my shoulder to someone and not talk to them at all. There are a few who are a little inebriated and start jabbering at you, and sometimes you get blindsided by someone who is really drunk and trying to ask you about how the offensive line is going to be next year.

When that happens, I am like, "Hey, man, it's February. I am just trying to relax, too." All you can do is kind of laugh about it. But sometimes you will get some older men who really follow the team closely, and they start listing off names and asking how this guy is doing or how that guy is doing. It's like they know more than I do, apparently. But for the most part about 99 percent of the people are really courteous and they just want to say hi and move on.

— ◆ —

Liam Kirby, Reesing's roommate, said, "Todd always handled it. I have never seen Todd ever lose his cool with fans, with people his age. But a lot of times you will get people who expect more of a relationship out of him when they have no reason to. They expect just because he is out at The Hawk or at Quinton's, they sort of expect him to be their best friend.
"To me it was almost annoying to have to stand there and wait for him to get done talking to whatever fan came up to him. When it is a little kid or someone who is gracious and wants to say 'Good to see you, congratulations on everything' it is fine. But there are those people who want to quiz him. I was with Todd because he was my friend and we ran around in the same circles. It wasn't became he was playing football. I didn't go to a football game until my senior year in college. I was working every weekend."

— ◆ —

On campus

The place where the least number of people came up to me was on campus. When I was walking through campus, people would never really stop me. I mean, everyone is going to class, and they don't want to stop someone when there are just hundreds of people walking around. So I never really had someone come up to me on campus or in the business school.

—◆—

Finance Professor Lisa Bergeron said other students sometimes weren't even aware Todd was in their classes. "He blends right in, so a lot of people didn't recognize him at first. They would be sitting by him and be talking about something going on with the football team and not even know he was sitting right next to them. Well, the girls definitely knew who he was. But a lot of times the guys had no idea. I would say he tried to not stand out by using his name. Now he is not a wallflower. He is boisterous and funny and stuff. But he never did that in the context of trying to let people know that he was Todd Reesing, quarterback.

"The first class he took from me, I knew there was a Todd Reesing, but I didn't know which student he was of the 500 or 600 in the class. A person I thought was Todd was asleep in class one day and I said something about it when he called me. He said, 'I was not asleep.' One of my TAs said, no the guy sleeping was not Todd, this other student was Todd."

—◆—

Students would come up to me, but it was more-so at other places, restaurants or at a bar or at a store when I was shopping. But not so much on campus. All the people who I was in class with, if they wanted to say something they would say it before or after class in passing. But they weren't going to hassle me because they knew I was going to be in class the next day or in two days and they would see me again.

*Bergeron said, "I will say this. When he was a TA, there
were more girls coming in for help on assignments than usual.
And I had several try to get his phone number from me. They would say,
'I am working with Todd on a group project, and I really need
to get in touch with him.' I would always tell them, I am happy to take
your phone number and I will get in touch with him and pass the
message. I am sure they could have found his e-mail address.
They didn't want his e-mail. They wanted his number."*

— ◆ —

*Kirby said, "It went one of two ways. Either people did not
recognize him at all — like they were totally unsuspecting of the
accomplishments and the responsibilities of who he was.
Or they recognized him immediately and they would barrage him
with things like drinks and too much attention and too many personal
questions. When all that Mangino stuff was going down, there were people
trying to get the inside scoop. That was just so tedious. I mean, no one
comes up to you if you work at a bank and says,
'I heard your boss is embezzling some money. Tell me about
that.' But he handled it graciously and with poise."*

— ◆ —

Hanging out

Football players pretty much do the same thing that all college students do. I mean, if you were hanging out in bars five nights a week, you are probably not going to be in the best shape. During the season so much of our time is taken up with football, that getting rest was too important to me to be hanging out all the time.

But young athletes, with all the stress we have, still like to have our fun. If you don't have some fun and get away from it, you might go crazy. Kids in college are still kids in college whether we are athletes or not. We still want to have some fun, so we did what everyone else does.

I know there is a statistic that athletes are more likely to be binge drinkers than other students. We always got the alcohol and drug talks from people who would give us all the facts. Their definition is something like two drinks in an hour. Under that standard, almost every college kid who goes out on a night is binge drinking. So I don't see how they say athletes are more prone to binge drinking. If everyone is binge drinking when they go out, then people who are going out more are binge drinking more. So I think their stats are a little off.

I was a social member of Phi Delta Theta. We had some guys on the team my first years who were Phi Delts. I lived next door to a couple of the guys on the team who were in the fraternity. We became friends, so I started meeting a lot of guys from the fraternity on the weekends and other stuff. I got initiated as a social member. I wasn't going to live there and didn't have to go through a pledgeship. But I was still associated with the house.

And I did other stuff with the house. After the Orange Bowl, John Larson and I were speakers at a Phi Delta Theta reunion thing in the Kansas City area just talking about being associated with the fraternity and football and things like that. So you get to meet a lot of the alums and things.

I know what we normally think of about fraternities. But it's also a way to meet other guys who go into business and whose parents have connections. So it's another way to network and meet some other good friends. All the guys are big sports fans. So I made a lot of friends through the fraternity, guys I will keep in touch with for years to come. So now, in addition to the great friends I have from football, I have friends from that, too.

The dating scene

Everyone has their perception of being the quarterback and being this and that ...

I never really had any serious girlfriends in college. I just didn't feel like I had the time for it. It's actually kind of funny because older people always ask if I have a girlfriend, or older players ... I would say, "No." And they would always say, "Keep it that way. You don't need that added stress."

The last thing you needed on a Thursday or Friday night when you have a big game on Saturday is your girlfriend yelling at you. You never want that.

—◆—

Kirby, who met Reesing at a Delta Upsilon party the first semester Reesing was at KU, said, "I think he had a serious girlfriend right after he got up here. But I think he found out she was dating his name and not dating him."

—◆—

I had a lot of girls who were friends at college that I just hung out with. I guess you could say I casually dated. But I hung out with a lot of girls who were good friends. I guess that was good enough for me, having some good friends and dating some people here and there.

It was always easier to go out on a date or meet someone in the off-season because you could take someone out on the weekends or this and that. You can't really go out on a date or go meet someone on Friday night when you have to get up the next day and have a game. And Saturday my parents were here for every game. So after games I would go home and hang out with them or friends who came into town. We would go out and eat and have fun after that.

My parents have met plenty of girls who are my friends. I lived next door to a couple who were good friends this past season. I have a friend from Austin, who is in school up here. Our families kind of knew each other, and I have met all her friends from her sorority. So my parents have met all sorts of girls I have been friends with.

There hasn't been any "Mom and Dad, this is my girlfriend and her name is . . ." conversation yet. We will wait until down the road when I bring a girl home to speak to Mom and Dad.

Jake Sharp said his second encounter with Reesing was a social one following the spring game of Reesing's freshman year. "I was still in high school, and he was the college boy or whatever. I met him at the recruiting game, and then I got in touch with him when he was in spring practice, and he said I should come up to the spring game and 'We'll go out afterwards and get some babes.' Did it happen? Oh, of course, of course (laughter). Me and Todd running the streets together ... it's game over. Game over. We had a good time at 18 years of age. I was still in high school thinking we were pretty cool."

—◆—

Social networking

I had a Facebook page my freshman year and halfway through my sophomore year. As soon as we started having success, then people from other schools started sending hate messages, cussing me out and saying all kinds of ungodly things. People I didn't even know were saying stuff all over the place. That's when I gave it the axe. I deleted it, and I haven't had one since 2007.

What is funny is that I had to come up to the athletic department about a year ago because someone was posing as me on Facebook. People I hadn't talked to in a while were writing things on this person's wall, and it wasn't even me. What was funny is that all the stuff up there was straight out of the media guide, and all the photos were just football pictures.

Now there are a couple of pages out there, but I don't think it is an actual profile page — at least it wasn't the last time I had my friend check for me. I don't really bother with it any more.

Twitter — I have never even looked at that.

The coaches never said you couldn't have one of those Facebook or MySpace pages (his last log-in to MySpace was November 2007). It was more a caution, "Just be smart about what you say out there because anybody can look at it. If you put something on there, realize the whole world is seeing what you are saying." If you put a quote out there that is disrespectful or something bad about someone, people are going to find out and know that you said it. So they constantly talked to us about being smart about that stuff.

I thought it was a lot easier not to have one and not worry about it. I just didn't want to have to deal with it. I never used it much anyway, so I didn't want to deal with people sending over stuff like that from other schools.

And, yeah, I just didn't have time for it. I had better things to do. If I have free time I would rather watch TV than surf Facebook. My roommate does it enough for both of us.

The competitive spirit

Sharp says Reesing was driven to win — and has been since he has known him, "I don't care what you are doing: badminton, beer pong. Whatever you are doing, the guy has got to win. He had this competitive streak. I don't have it. I am like, 'Whatever,' if it's anything competition-wise. He had this game in the locker room. I think it was Orange Bowl year. They would throw Gatorade bottles into different trash cans through the room. He would play it every day; it was a serious competition."

—◆—

It was called G-Rade bottle-toss. Aqib (Talib) named it, actually. We had teams. What we would do before every practice is pick a different spot in the locker room. You would have to toss a Gatorade bottle into a trash can. We would keep a running tally, and at the end of the season whatever team lost would have to buy the other one food and drinks out on the town. The first year, Adam (Barmann) and I beat Aqib and Gary Green. We stomped them. The next year, Derek (Fine) and I won against Gary Green and someone else. We swept them. It wasn't even close.

In 2009, we were at a new facility, and it just wasn't the same. The new locker room ... plus everyone I had played with, everyone else was gone. So it would have been against rookies. No G-Rade bottle toss.

—◆—

Fine said, "He always wants to win. Most of our group of friends were like that."

—◆—

Dicus, his high school coach, said, "I think the competitiveness and the inner drive that Todd has really stemmed through his entire life. The way he was at Kansas was exactly how he was at Lake Travis, a great leader, great personality-type kid. He understands what his priorities are in life."

A regular guy

Todd has made and maintained friendships throughout his life. He has stayed close with a group of high school friends — none of whom attended his high school. He has kept in touch with former teammates. And he has the ability to cut through age barriers from grade-schoolers to alums.

— ♦ —

Adrian Mayes, a former teammate, says, "I don't know how to explain it. Guys just gravitate toward him. He always likes to joke around and things of that sort. But he is also always so overly happy. He is relaxed and loose. I think that might be his best attribute as a quarterback.

"Quarterback is a weird position. I have never played it, but I have heard Coach say they want somebody back there who is loose and can handle the pressure. His personality was loose, laid back ... a cool type of guy. That helped him and enabled us to get through big games when we were down or something. He was able to stay calm and tell the guys it would be all right. But besides being a good football player, he is just a very good person."

— ♦ —

Sanguily said, "Everybody always loved him. He just projects this feeling about him that you just want to be around. He is always trying to have fun. But more importantly, he cares that everyone around him is having fun. It's always been that way — even since before girls or people really paid attention to sports."

— ♦ —

Former KU quarterback John Hadl said, "He has some real people skills. I didn't really have too much interaction with him until after the season this year. We had one of our alums who has a couple of boys, 10 and 12, I think. Of course Todd is their idol. I asked Todd if he would meet them in the parking lot and shake their hands.

"He said, 'Sure.' These kids don't know he's coming, and when he walks up their eyes are big as saucers. They shook his hand and all that, and he was really talking great to them about what they did and how they did it. It was in a parking lot west of the stadium. I told him I had a football out in my car, and he ought to throw them a few passes. He said sure and fired off about 30 passes to those two little boys. He was running their tails off. They couldn't believe it. That was a pretty cool experience for those two boys."

—◆—

Finance professor Lisa Bergeron watched Reesing's interaction with her sons and the PTA at their school, saying, "We're talking to one of my TAs who moved to New York, and he lives in this area where he was approached by prostitutes. I said, 'Speaking of prostitutes, Todd, I have a question for you.' He is like, what are you talking about? I said, 'I want to whore you out to the PTA, I want to auction you off.' So we auction him off, and there were probably 30 kids at the park when he came and he was playing football with them.

"He made sure every kid got at least one catch. He could remember in his head, which ones had and hadn't. If one was a little more awkward, he could relate to that, and if a kid dropped a pass it was, 'Oh, that was my fault.' He made them all feel like they were special and they were great athletes. He can reach kids and knows how to talk to them. He doesn't baby talk them, but talks to them like a person. They appreciate that.

"And he's fantastic around the parents. He can go from talking to my son, Mikey (5 years old), to talking to a 45-year-old. His interpersonal skills are amazing. And afterwards, he said, 'I really had a good time.'"

She also saw his leadership qualities away from the football field. "When we were grading exams, there are 600, 700 exams, and we would grade them at night. All the TAs would be sitting around the room. He could sense when the mood was about to shift and you were getting tired or burned out or starting to complain. He would rally the troops with a joke or put his hat on backwards and say, 'Let's dig in and get this done.' I was always appreciative when I could see him realizing it and it was like, 'You do this, this and this and we are going to be out of here.' He could really rally them."

—◆—

Longtime friend Andrew Williamson said, "Todd is one of those guys who is really hard to not get along with. He is a really likeable guy. When our group of friends gets together, I am always worried about something or stressed out that something won't work out. But Todd is always along for the ride. We all have something of the same personalities and we all like to make fun of each other. He's funny. Sometimes Todd wears some just outlandish stuff. So we make fun of him like that. He always takes it pretty well."

———◆———

Patrick Sanguily, a childhood friend, said, "He could have been like, 'I'm going to decide what we are going to do because I am leading this entourage and people will recognize me and we might get more benefits.' But he never does anything like that, which is just kind of who he is. He is all about everything being a great situation and everyone being happy and carefree. Whenever he is with me or Andrew or Kevin, he is always, 'Hey, I am going to let you guys decide what to do because I know you will care way more than I do. I just want to hang out with you guys.' It's funny that he usually lets us call the shots because he knows he is going to have a good time no matter what."

———◆———

Former teammate and roommate Derek Fine said, "You can't help just wanting to be around him. He always wants to win, but that's kind of the way most of our group of friends were. Just watching him play makes the game exciting for you when you see him shake three guys, lose about 25 yards and then come running back closer to the line and flinging that bitch 40 yards off balance or off one foot.

"Not only is he my friend, which I take a lot of pride in, he's almost like one of my little brothers or something. He sometimes isn't really good at comebacks. When he was living with James (Holt) and me, we would just start eating at him when he would do something that kind of irritated us. He would be sitting there and look at us and not be able to think of anything to say. Then it was, 'Screw you guys,' and he would roll over on the couch."

———◆———

Former teammate and roommate James Holt says, "It was always fun rooming with him and Derek because we would always be reaming on each other. One day it would be me and Todd ganging up on Derek, then the other way. It was always fun. It was kind of unfair because me and Derek are Oklahoma kids and Todd is a Texas kid. So it wasn't fair for him."

— ◆ —

Kirby says Todd is a neat-freak. "He is compulsively cleaning all the time. When we lived in the older house it was much more apparent. But if you look in his closet, it would have been organized by color, whether it was button down, long sleeve. All organized. Everything taken into account and organized in that fashion. Everything was always put away clean and organized."

One of his high school friends says he was such a perfectionist in his appearance that the color of his T-shirt under the polo shirt had to match the logo. "I have seen that," says Kirby. He is very much Southern fraternity style in his clothing options. He's very meticulous."

— ◆ —

Kirby says he had only one complaint as Todd's roommate. "The guy likes one kind of music. The techno doesn't end until like 5 in the morning on Saturdays, Sundays, Mondays and Tuesday. You gotta like techno to live with Todd. Tiesto nonstop. I can't tell you how many times I have heard the CD "Elements of Life." "Adagio for Strings" is the track he prefers. He actually tried to get it as the kickoff music at the KU games. Actually I did see him change up. He also listens to Dave Matthews. He knows every word to every Dave Matthews song I have ever heard. But I think that was a high school thing, and when he came to college he was really getting into techno. He even does some of his own mixes. It's not the smoothest work I have ever heard, but he's getting there."

— ◆ —

Ashmos cites another example of Reesing being a normal college guy, saying, "Three or four days after the Orange Bowl I asked him to come visit at SMU. I was like, 'Hey, we have our rush week at SMU.' He said, 'Oh, I'll come up there.' He came up and stayed at the fraternity house and was just *hanging out. These freshmen recruits who were going through rush, about five or six of them, would say, 'Is that Todd Reesing? I just saw him in the Orange Bowl. What's he doing playing pool with his shirt off down at the frat house in SMU?' That's just another example of how he was one of the guys."*

Elvis has left the building

Ashmos and Sanguily, two of Todd's life-long friends, were stunned at how popular Reesing was at Kansas when they came to Lawrence to games. "It was crazy," said Ashmos. "I have been around Texas athletes and have seen those guys at parties. But they were nothing like Todd. They didn't socialize like Todd did. They don't really mix with other students. Todd was just another student. And I had no idea how big he was there. He is really modest, and he would never tell you he was Elvis up there, but he was. It was crazy."

The Future **11**

I've had some time to reflect since the end of the season. Playing in the East-West Shrine game didn't turn out quite the way I wanted it to because it didn't help me get invited to the NFL Combine. At the pro day we had at KU, I really didn't get a chance to throw as many passes as I would have liked to.

So it really hurts that my career is over at KU. Going out the way we did with seven straight losses really sucked, too. But it didn't douse my desire to continue playing football. So that's what I'm going to try to do. I've beaten the odds before when most college recruiters told me I was too little to play for them in Division I. So I will try to beat the odds again. I'm used to it.

I signed with the Saskatchewan Roughriders of the Canadian Football League in May and went north for a quarterback camp. When I agreed to their contract, I thought there were going to be four guys to compete for three spots. Their starter is Darian Durant, who led them to the Grey Cup last year. They had two other guys, neither of whom had played in the CFL. So I thought I would have a pretty good shot. Then the same day they signed me, they also brought in a fifth quarterback: Ryan Dinwiddie.

Dinwiddie had played for Saskatchewan's offensive coordinator last year when both were with Winnipeg. So it seemed pretty clear that the OC up there wanted him. So now there was one spot for three guys. I was released after two days of training camp.

For now, my "future" is undecided. But we'll always keep looking ahead.

When my agent and I were talking to them, we signed with the understanding I was going to be given a chance to compete and go through all of training camp without the possibility I would get cut. When I met with Brendan Taman (General Manager of the Roughriders), he was all, "Oh, I never saw this coming. I really thought you were going to be here with us. If I thought this was going to happen, I would have never had you come up here."

Whatever ... I guess in business that kind of stuff happens. You are not guaranteed anything, and they don't owe you anything.

I was there for the rookie minicamp and two days of training camp. I got to throw the ball only five days. I knew I wasn't going to blow them away with throwing one-on-one. When I did get in the live team settings and it was more like a game when you would be running eight or nine plays in a row, we were moving the ball.

Basically, what it came down to is this: they didn't know if my arm was strong enough or something like that, size, whatever. I think the GM was kind of the only one who really knew what my skills fit. I doubt their coaches had even seen me play in college or that I was the kind of player if you give him a chance to play in a game it would be a whole different thing.

But they only have one week of training camp before their first game, and they wanted to get the number down real fast. I had hoped that I would get a chance to at least play in the first preseason game and show them what I can do. I've never been the guy who is going to wow you in one-on-ones, but if you watched any games over the last four years with Kansas, you know that I know how to make plays and play the game. Unfortunately, I didn't get to show it.

But at the end of the day, it's not my decision. I did the best I could. I thought I showed my mobility pretty well, but even that is hard in practice because they blow the whistle when anybody gets close to you. If I had a chance to play in the first game, I think it might have been different. I think I might have shown something you can't show in practice.

Ken Miller, Saskatchewan's head coach, told reporters,
"It was a close battle, but we had to make a decision for the good
of the team. It wasn't so much that Todd was the odd man out, it was the
others were in. We only have (practice) repetitions that are available for
four. When you throw a fifth into the mix, it's really tough for the
top four to get reps and get the work they need."

— ◆ —

Doug Berry, the offensive coordinator, told reporters,
"In the long run, we knew that Darian was our quarterback.
We knew Ryan was the most experienced and a viable
No. 2. Cole Bergquist has been here in the past and has a really
strong arm. We decided to go with Kent (Smith) because of his
height (6'5"), speed and his arm strength."

— ◆ —

I think I have enough size because I was only a little bit shorter than Darian. I may not have as strong an arm as his but I was able to complete most of my passes. I may not be able to throw it 70 yards on a rope but as camp went on I think I would have been able to complete the passes I was asked to. Just because I believe it doesn't mean someone else does. I didn't do enough to change their opinion.

I guess I will look at the United Football League. They have a team in Omaha. I had decided to go to the CFL because it was an established league that has a lot of fan support. After being up there, the style of play would have been right up my alley. You are in the shotgun all the time, rolling out a little bit, throwing the ball. I think it would have been a great fit.

I'm really disappointed about the CFL experience because I thought I was going into a situation where they seemed really excited about having me up there. It was kind of like with Coach Mangino. I didn't have to prove stuff to him or go to a tryout camp with him or anything like that. He thought I was a good fit and that was enough. Same thing with Saskatchewan.

Brendan Taman, the general manager, had been looking
forward to seeing Reesing in person. Saskatchewan had him on
its negotiation list since 2007. "One of the things I envy about the people
from the NFL is that they have six weeks of training camp. We come in
and have seven days before we play our first exhibition game. When you
are coming up as a quarterback, the CFL is a different world, and it can be
a pretty eye-opening experience with the nuances of the extra player, the
wider field, the time between plays. Just realistically, if we had six weeks of
training camp and a couple of minicamps, he would have had a
better chance to make a real impression.

"He was the kind of player who wouldn't pass the NFL eye-check
test in his physical stature, which in our league we don't care about
that as much. We care about how he makes plays."

—◆—

It's funny that he would have said that before I went up there. When I met with him he said, "You kind of got NFL-ed, got cut based upon purely physical attributes, not the intangibles and what you could do on the field but what you look like." It really seemed like it was more an evaluation based on size and arm strength than on whether you could make plays and move the chains.

I haven't heard anything from any other CFL team. Being on Saskatchewan's negotiating list meant that they were the only ones I could negotiate with. If something happened, I would love to go back up there because, like I said, the style of play really fits what I do.

Now I will probably try to give the UFL a shot. They don't even start training camp up until August, but I am sure there are a lot of open quarterback spots. Some of those teams want to see who gets cut from NFL camps and things like that. But I will try to get an invitation to a camp in the UFL and maybe try to make that happen. We really hadn't talked about that much because we never really thought this was coming. So we'll see if I can get on somewhere and get another chance. If not, then on to graduate school.

It's not that I want to continue playing football because I will get rich doing it. And it's not because I feel like I have to prove that I can continue playing football. I don't think I have to prove that at all. It's what I enjoy doing. Football is still fun. I am still young. My body is not too banged up from the last four years. I still feel like I can go out there and compete. And it would be a lot of fun to keep on playing and go to some new places and play with some new guys. We will see how it goes.

The NFL experience

It was a little frustrating to not be invited to the NFL Combine to at least get a chance to throw for NFL scouts. And at our pro day at KU, I think I only got to throw 20 or 25 passes. I was expecting to get to throw all the routes that you would throw in the NFL, and I had prepared to do that. But it's not really up to you. Whatever scouts are there, whatever they want, then that's what they will have you do. They are running it. You are just there.

You do the standard tests that everyone does, but when it comes to position stuff they kind of leave that and once they have seen what they want, then that's it. There were quite a few of our guys there, probably about 12 guys because some of the older guys came back and worked out, too. But it seems like the scouts already had their minds made up that I was too short no matter what I was doing on the field. If they really have no interest in watching you throw that much, then that's it.

I hoped the East-West game would make an impression on them. And compared with the other guys, I thought I had pretty solid practices. The hardest thing there is that you don't practice very long. So you are not taking very many reps. So it's hard to get into a rhythm. You are getting maybe six or seven reps in seven-on-sevens and maybe six or seven reps in teamwork. Probably half of those are run plays. So you are really only throwing nine or 10 passes in the whole practice against live competition.

You have a different group of receivers in there every time you go. Each receiver runs routes differently. Their speed is different, and you don't have a chance to develop any timing. So from that aspect it's tough to get on the same page with guys and find a rhythm. A lot of times being a quarterback is all about finding that rhythm and getting into synch.

But for the most part, I didn't have any trouble going under center, taking snaps, taking drops. None of that was an issue. I thought I handled that just fine. For the limited amount of stuff we were allowed to do, I thought I showcased some good stuff. It wasn't perfect, but no one was at any position.

I actually watched almost all of the draft to see where some of our guys at Kansas were drafted. I was interested in that. But, realistically, I didn't think I would be picked.

It makes it a little easier to deal with because I know that they have these perceptions that you have to be this tall and weigh this much or you have to have some sort of undefined arm strength. There are plenty of guys who have really strong arms who can't complete a 6-yard slant. That doesn't do their team a whole lot of good.

—◆—

Steve Reesing said, "We had low expectations that he would be drafted because we were not having any communication with anybody during this process. So we went in not expecting to be drafted. We were hopeful that someone would give him a chance and at a worst-case situation that he might get a free agent contract and be given a chance to prove himself."

—◆—

I hoped that Drew Brees' success might have opened a few eyes that you don't have to fit the exact prototype. He has had tremendous success throughout his whole career. He does dropbacks. He does play-actions. He gets in the guns. And it's not like the Saints offensive line is blocking different and he's doing a lot of different things in the pocket.

His whole career he has learned to find the throwing lanes, just like I have had to do. He knows that sometimes you have to slide one way or throw it with a little different arm angle or this and that. The NFL is so much based on timing and being at the right location,

I am sure he throws the ball a lot of times without ever seeing the receiver.

I did that all the time in college. You expect the receiver to be in the right spot and do his job. If you throw the ball on time and to the right location and he is there, it all works out. It takes out some of the "having to always see it" or having a great view because you're standing up taller and looking over everyone. And it really doesn't matter if you are 6'2" or 6'3". You still aren't going to see over those guys who are 6'6" anyway. Every quarterback knows it is not about seeing over the big tackles, it is about seeing throwing lanes around them.

—◆—

Reesing is getting encouragement from his family, especially brother Kyle. Kyle's baseball career was over before it began because of injuries and job opportunities. "He talked to me a lot about it. My thought is that if the passion and attitude is still there and you want to continue playing, then keep playing. At some point you won't be able to, but at least you can say, 'Hey, I took my shot.' He's got the rest of his life to work. There's a short window to pursue this football thing. Obviously, the odds are against him. There is the stereotype of guys that now-days for a quarterback to be successful they have to be 6'3" or taller. That's a preconceived notion ingrained in the football community. Guys are overlooked because of one factor, and that is height. But game films don't lie. People should focus more on productivity and what a player can do."

—◆—

High school friend Kevin Ashmos puts it more succinctly: "I don't think he is any different than any of the quarterbacks who went out this year other than height. He's a better thrower than Tebow. He has a stronger arm than McCoy, and I think he is smarter and throws better than Jimmy Clausen. So I guess it is 3 inches that separates him from making $40 million and trying to get picked up somewhere. Guys like Ryan Leaf, who is 6'5" and had one good bowl game, get $20 million and play five games and retire. JaMarcus Russell ... those guys are big. It just doesn't mean anything."

—◆—

It's a little hard to accept knowing that my future opportunities to play football were going to purely come down to size. My future is not going to come down to what my footwork is or how I understand offensive or defensive schemes. It was all going to come down to my size.

Other people would say you could change their perception, but the reality is if I were bigger — with the productivity I had in college — we wouldn't be having a discussion on why. No matter what my football skills, there wasn't anything that was going to make me taller or throw the ball 75 yards.

— ◆ —

Former KU receiver Derek Fine spent two seasons with the Buffalo Bills. He says Reesing is plenty good enough to play in the NFL. "Obviously, I am going to be a little bit biased. Whenever I was in Buffalo, I felt like Todd was better than any of the quarterbacks I played with there — more about playing football. Trent Edwards has an unbelievable set of skills, just unrealistic. Some of the throws I have seen him make in practice, I would just say, 'Wow, I can't believe that just happened.' But we get in a game, and that wasn't there. The difference between them and Todd is whenever Todd got into the game, he was going to show up and play. He wasn't going to get frustrated. He wasn't going to lose his composure. That's what separates him from other quarterbacks. The kid can play football. If you look at him, it's like, 'Who's this little frat-boy dude walking around in his Ray-Bans and his Croakies?' But when it comes to game time, the kid can play."

— ◆ —

Coach Mark Mangino, who overlooked Reesing's size when he offered Todd a scholarship, says Reesing has other factors. "He's got football savvy. He's got the 'IT' factor you are looking for in a quarterback. If the play breaks down, he can still make plays. You break a defense's back when it does everything right and they've got you and all of a sudden the quarterback makes a play. That's what he brings to that football team."

— ◆ —

Former KU linebacker James Holt, now with the San Diego Chargers, said, "Most definitely he could play in the NFL. He has a strong arm. He is accurate. The only thing that stopped him from getting drafted or picked up is his size. Most NFL scouts look for the bigger quarterbacks now. You look at JaMarcus Russell and you can see how that worked out. I don't see the logic to it. If you can play the game, you can play the game."

—◆—

Former KU running back Jake Sharp, fighting the same size battle to get into the NFL, said, "We are plenty good enough to play. We are not the measurables, but I guarantee you we are a lot better than some guys playing in the NFL. They forget about what makes a football player. I went to a tryout during a Bears rookie camp. Todd could hold his weight with any of them. So it's very unsettling how the NFL looks at things. I can't stress enough that it's what's in a player's heart, what's in their soul."

—◆—

I guess the reason I am not totally freaked out about what happened is because I was pretty realistic about how it would all work. It's just like anything, the NFL, any sports league, is about perceptions. "This is the way it's going to be, this is the way it's going to happen." They don't like to break the mold and do new things. That is just not their style. People's livelihoods are at stake, so they are not going to take chances.

I had a pretty small percentage that there was even a chance I might get invited to a minicamp or picked up as a free agent. But I was also pretty realistic that there was a pretty good chance it was not going to happen. So when it didn't, I'm not sitting here saying, "This is so screwed up. Look at what I did in college. Why didn't I get a chance? I know I am short and this and that … "

—◆—

Dicus said, "You always hear of these stories of guys who make it in the NFL going, 'Gosh, can you believe it?' I don't know if there is a better example than Drew Brees. You can go around to every team and there are guys who have his size, the same type of heart and the competitiveness he has within him. I would put money down that if given a chance, Todd would be able to do some good things."

—◆—

This is kind of what I expected. I still worked hard to get ready for the pro day and do the best I could. You can only show what you did in college and then do good on your pro day. But at a certain point, these general managers and scouts were saying, "OK, but he's still only this tall and this big."

———◆———

Debi Reesing said, "As a parent, you always want to do anything you can to support your child so he could achieve his goals. That was a dream and aspiration for Todd. So we wanted that for him as well. But he had made some comments that I think he was trying to prepare himself and us at the same time so that there wouldn't be big expectations. But you feel bad for a kid who's talented and won't even get a shot or an invitation to a free agent camp.

"That's why he wasn't recruited a lot out of high school. Nobody thought he would be able to play in college, he would never be able to throw over those linemen. Well guess what? In a lot of ways Todd dispelled that. It's not about the height, it's about getting a shot. That's kind of what happened at KU. You put some players around Todd, and Todd can make it happen. He just has a head and eyes for the football field."

———◆———

Getting a chance to play football after college anywhere is really a blessing for anyone. The way I look at it, it would be nice to get a chance to make an NFL team, but at the same time, just getting a chance to play football would be fun.

"I wouldn't bet against the kid."

Former NFL coach Marty Schottenheimer coached Reesing in the East-West All-Star game following the 2009 season. Schottenheimer also coached Drew Brees, who stands just six feet tall, when they were with the San Diego Chargers.

"When you make a decision, you look at the whole picture, and he has some very definite positive qualities. You need to know going in what the limitations are. Could he be an exception? Yeah, he might be because of his competitiveness.

"He is very, very bright. He picks up concepts very quickly. He is very intuitive. But his height is going to be

the one thing everybody is looking at.

"I really liked the kid. He is competitive and he is smart.
He has really good instincts. Guys who have natural instincts for the
game, their development can come much quicker than a guy who has to
learn his way. "He doesn't have a rocket for an arm, but it is certainly
good enough. You don't have to have a rocket arm, look at Drew (Brees).
To me, it's nice to have a guy with a strong arm. But I'll tell you
what, I would rather have a guy who didn't have a strong arm and
had the ability to throw the touch passes and had the accuracy as
opposed to a guy who is slinging the ball all over the place.
"His lack of height is going to be the thing he has to overcome, and
that would mean mastering all the other skills. Then there is the
possibility he could play and he could beat the height limitation.
"It's hard, when you see all the things he has done and the success
he has had, to say the height limitation is going to be his Achilles heel.
The reality of it is that height is the problem. But I will say this, if
you give him a chance, he would be a hard guy to get rid of because
you want that kind of guy around your program."

The time frame

I haven't really set a limit to how long I will keep trying to chase the dream of playing. As long as I want to play and as long as I enjoy doing it and my body is healthy enough, then I will keep doing it. I have a whole life and plenty of decades after this that I am going to be able to do business or work. So while I am young and while I can, I might as well keep playing.

I'll probably try to work on my MBA in the off-season, working on it a semester at a time. That is something I will give some thought to. I had a chance to apply to be a Rhodes Scholar. Lew Perkins, our athletic director, talked to me about it. I met with some counselors at the honors college, and we talked about it and what it entails and what would go into it and all of that.

I was on the verge of beginning the process to apply. One of the things that you do, if you get through the first few rounds of elimination, is go to an interview. It's on a Saturday, and they won't reschedule it. They looked up the date, and the interview would have been on the Saturday we played Texas in Austin. If I had made the final interview — which to have made it that far would have been unbelievable and would have been a big if — but I wasn't going to be put in that spot.

And by that time, I had started thinking that maybe I did want to keep playing football. If I had received the Rhodes Scholarship it wouldn't have done me a whole lot of good to take a whole year off and put off my chances to keep playing football. I would have missed that opportunity. The education is always going to be there, but football you may get one opportunity, and I wanted to max that out.

I haven't really given a lot of thought to what I want to do after playing football. My brother is an analyst for a private equity firm and he lives in New York.

— ◆ —

"He definitely doesn't see himself working behind a desk," Kyle said. "Personally, I think he'd like to work as a trader. You get that locker-room atmosphere working on the trading floor with a bunch of guys. It's high intensity from market's open to market's close. You're going, going, going."

— ◆ —

I do agree that I need a little more action, but I don't know where he gets the idea I would want to be on the floor of the exchange. That sounds absolutely terrible. That sounds like high stress, just way too much. I'm all about being active, and I can't just be bottled up in an office. But I am a low-stress kind of person. I am easy going.

I could see myself wanting to do something internationally while I am still relatively young and get a chance to maybe travel more and do some business overseas and stuff like that.

One of the things that happens when you play football at a big university is that you do get to meet a lot of alumni and people associated with the school or the athletic department. A lot of them are in business in a position where they might be able to help young people. They see that I studied finance and econ and that I wanted to get into business.

It's not so much that they want to offer you a job or anything, but several expressed a willingness to help find things, sort of saying, "Hey, I know you want to play football and want to do this or that. But if there is ever any way I can help you with anything or you need a reference for a job or a contact, don't hesitate to give me a call.

The legacy they left

In 2006, my first year, you had a few hard core football fans and the families at the away games.

By 2007, I think it was after we beat Kansas State. The next week we were at Colorado, we had a lot of KU fans at the Colorado game. When we got to A&M, it just got bigger and bigger. Everywhere we went we had more and more fans. Same with the home games. The preseason we didn't sell out the games. But we kept winning and winning, and then we got into Big 12 play. Those last home games (Iowa State and Nebraska), those were both sellouts and people were packed on the hill.

You could see the transformation from my first start. I don't know, 45,000 — a lot of seats open. You start winning and people are getting more and more excited. It just escalated.

— ◆ —

Meier said, "Our contribution is going to be viewed in an assortment of ways, but for me it will always be that we were part of the group that got KU going. Our senior class isn't necessarily the one that put KU on the map because there are a lot of guys who helped build a very solid foundation when we started: you think about guys like Brandon McAnderson, Derek Fine, guys like that. They are the guys who really set the foundation of what KU football was all about — hard work and being blue-collar guys and out-working people.

"At KU, honestly, we don't get the best athletes or blue-chip guys coming out of high school. We get a bunch of hard-working guys who earn their way, guys who will be there to work and work hard day in and day out. We were a part of that group that definitely

helped the program get touted. But there were a lot of guys in the years previous to mine and Darrell and Jake and Todd who made serious commitments to establish KU football.

"There will be a bunch of people who view it that the seniors were part of 2009 when Coach Mark Mangino was fired for his actions and stuff like that. People can view it how they want. But I am going to view it that I was part of something great and helped the KU program take the right steps in the direction they want to get. We are close to where they want to get and where Coach (Turner) Gill wants to get. But we laid the foundation"

—◆—

Debi Reesing said she is proud of her son. "I am proud that he helped give some validity in this decade of football for KU. They had some great All-America players come through their program. But in this decade, he helped spark the fans and alumni to return and support that team. I know what the games were like his freshman year, so I had at least that comparison. But when he was there, KU people were excited about football. I know he is proud of his university, and I think he is proud of his contributions to the football program, and we're proud of it, too. We're very proud."

—◆—

My parents, Steve and Debi, attended the National Football Foundation awards dinner following the 2009 season.

Lew Perkins says, "They raised the bar higher than anybody would ever have expected at that particular time. I tried to separate what was going on in our football program (investigation of Mangino) from our kids. I tried to keep them out of it as much as I could. I know what a commitment they all made and what a commitment they made to themselves and their football teammates. It is hard to watch when you have such high expectations. It's hard. Not only Todd, but all that class, they never quit. They always showed up for practice. They always showed up for games. I'll always have a great deal of respect for them for that — not only the seniors but all of them.
"In 2007 when we started winning a lot of games, I don't think anyone saw that coming. I don't want to tell you I saw that coming. I knew we had some great kids and knew we had some class kids. The coaching staff did a great job. Mark did a great job. It all clicked."

—◆—

Adrian Mayes, a guard on the 2007 and 2008 teams, said, "We always wanted to do something that somebody said we couldn't. A lot of times we were hearing from news people saying that we couldn't get it done or we're not good enough. We always wanted to prove somebody wrong, and we were able to do it."

—◆—

Looking ahead for the Jayhawks

I think the future of Kansas football is bright. The last few years we have built a foundation for success. People expect Kansas football to go to higher places and continue on what we built these last four or five years. The younger guys all realize that, and they are hungry. They are ready to get out there and continue to go to bowl games and compete for championships.

I had a chance to meet Coach (Turner) Gill and all the rest of the staff. They are a great group of guys. They are very motivational. They are encouraging, and I think the guys on the team are going to react well to them.

*Meier said, "One thing that really stood out for
me is that there was kind of a revived energy level. A lot of
guys are really excited to be out there. Spring practice is not the greatest
time of the year, and it is hard to get motivated to do things. But there was
a different feeling at practice than being at a practice with
Coach Mangino. There was definitely a little spark out there.
"They will be a young team, and everybody has a clean start to where they
are with the program and have a chance to establish themselves.
Even though Coach Gill hasn't coached any games yet, the things he has
done in the community and academics are really good. I am excited for
the guys because I know there is a lot of talent at KU right now and know
if they can put their hard work and their football game together, they are
going to have a good year."*

—◆—

There are going to be some growing pains at times. It is going to be tough for some of the younger guys to step into some pretty big shoes on offense and defense. But when they do step up and start making plays and come together and find their identity as a team, they are going to be really good, and the future holds some good things.

I know I am excited to watch them play. I can't wait to watch my first game in Memorial Stadium and not be on the sidelines. I am a proud alum, and I can't wait to watch these guys in the future and come back here for a few years to come. I hope I am playing in the fall for a few more years to come, but I am sure I could find a way to squeeze back for a game or two.

Memorable Plays

*T*here were plenty of plays during Todd Reesing's career that were memorable. His friend Kevin Ashmos believes the signature play came against Oklahoma State.

"The one play that kind of put him on the map was the play at Oklahoma State his sophomore year," Ashmos said. "I can hear (Brent) Musburger's voice, 'reminiscent of Doug Flutie.' He scrambled around, ran around, got back, kept going and found (Dexton) Fields. It was back-breaking for Oklahoma State. It was on national TV, and I was thinking now here is the national recognition."

Here's the call from Musburger and Kirk Herbstreit:

———◆———

Brent Musburger: "Here's Reesing. Picks up a block, still looking for someone, going hard to the right, avoids a tackle. Shades of Doug Flutie, then completes a pass to Dexton Fields. How about that. That would make Mr. Flutie proud back there in the studio."

Kirk Herbstreit: "I am sure Doug is watching along and probably moving. He is one of these guys who moves around when he watches a game. Todd Reesing is moving all over the pocket. He comes up, I thought he was going to take off. But he does a great job of keeping his focus down the field and throwing the football."

———◆———

Someone else may choose a play he made against South Florida in 2008 when he scrambled and then called his shot and connected with Johnathan Wilson in the end zone, described by Sean McDonough: "He is Fran Tarkenton the second."

Reesing has his own highlights, starting with the first time the red shirt was ripped from his back. The following are Reesing's choices in no particular order after the first.

Colorado, Oct. 28, 2006
63-yard run to the Colorado 1 in his first game

That was a run of 200 yards to gain 60 on a play, back-and-forth all over the field. *From the KU 25, Reesing takes snap from under center, drops back, slides left, then darts to the outside on the right when he is flushed from the pocket. He tucks the ball under his right arm and heads up field, switching the ball to his left arm and weaving back-and-forth for a 63-yard romp.*

Sam Houston State, Sept. 20, 2008
57-yard touchdown pass to Dezmon Briscoe

This is one of the favorite plays of my whole career — a 60-yard ball in the air that hit Briscoe in stride that ended up being the No. 1 play on ESPN that week. It was also on my 21st birthday. It was third-and-25. Nobody was open, I scrambled left, then back to my right, and hit him in stride with the throw.

Colorado, Oct. 20, 2007
Reesing 53-yard run on a broken play

It was a passing play that broke down. I faked a guy, and he jumped up and went past me. I remember Derek Fine blocked a cornerback for about 30 yards, just pushing him downfield. He was manhandling him, literally picked him up and carried him about 30 yards. So the two longest runs of my career came against Colorado.

Oklahoma State, Nov. 10, 2007
45-yard pass to Dexton Fields to the Oklahoma State 15

This play went on for about 13 seconds where I scramble left and right. If you watch my drop, you can see I am clearly favoring that left foot because of the high ankle sprain I had earlier in the game. I can't put any pressure on it, so it looks really unorthodox because I am trying not to use that foot. I wasn't looking to run on that play at all because my ankle was just killing me.

South Florida, Sept. 12, 2008
18-yard touchdown pass to Johnathan Wilson

That's definitely up there. We were behind. I scrambled back and then started running to the left when I kind of pointed to him and hit him in the end zone.

Nebraska, Nov. 8, 2008
28-yard touchdown pass to Kerry Meier

I took the snap from the shotgun and faked a run to the left. Then I was flushed from the pocket to the right and this linebacker just came up and belted me. But he didn't wrap up, and I bounce off him and stay on my feet. When you watch this play from the end-zone view, you can see Kerry lying on the ground when this dude drills me. Kerry looks almost like he is modeling with his hand cocked on the back of his helmet. When he sees I don't go down, he pops up and I hit him for the touchdown. I remember after I threw it, I didn't even get excited. But I stared the guy down and then just walked off. That's definitely one of my favorites.

---◆---

Meier said, "I can remember that one.
Once again, I pop up and go deep and he found me."

---◆---

Missouri, Nov. 29, 2008
28-yard winning touchdown to Kerry Meier

We have talked about this forever. But this stands out because of the circumstances. You want to have a chance with the ball with less than two minutes, against your biggest rival, with snow falling. You couldn't draw up the circumstances any better. I hadn't had a whole lot of chances to lead that kind of comeback. It was definitely the most exciting game I played the whole time at KU because of getting a chance to make that last-minute drive. People have told me that was the most exciting game they ever saw of KU football. To be a part of that and be a guy who helped make that last play.

— ◆ —

Meier said, "We just did what Todd did best, creating and making a play on the run. It was kind of a bang-bang play."

— ◆ —

Insight Bowl vs. Minnesota Dec. 31, 2008
80-yard touchdown pass to Dezmon Briscoe

This is kind of the way you want to start a game every time. The first play of the game, I got the snap in the shotgun and was looking for Dezmon Briscoe. I had to duck under a rusher, then scramble to my left. I didn't even get my body squared up to the line and just lofted it toward Briscoe, who took it 80 yards for the touchdown.

Duke, Sept. 19, 2009
17-yard scramble to Duke 4

There was a pass in that game that was good, but the run was real cool. It was a called pass play, but one of the D-linemen was coming at me. I started running, then I realized I wasn't going to get around him. I made a quick pivot and literally put my hand on the ground. The guy flew by and fell down. I spun around on my hand and took off and ran it all the way down to the 4-yard line.

Quick-Hitters with Todd

- **Favorite type of music:** Techno
- **Favorite song:** There are two: one is called "Feel Alive" by the Benassi Brothers. The other is "Adagio for Strings" by Tiesto.
- **Least favorite music:** Death metal. Never been a real fan of that.
- **Favorite artist:** Tiesto, a DJ
- **Favorite movie:** The movie is always tough for me. I like a lot of different movies. *Avatar* was awesome.
- **Favorite Actress:** I'm a big Scarlett Johansson fan.
- **Favorite Actor:** Leonardo DiCaprio. He's the man.
- **Favorite TV show:** "Dexter." It's on Showtime
- **Favorite video game:** I've never been a big video game player. The only one I have played in the last decade is FIFA World Cup. I haven't owned a video game console since I was a kid.
- **Favorite NFL team growing up:** The Cowboys
- **Favorite NFL team now:** At this point, I am a fan of whatever team my friends are playing on.
- **Favorite baseball team:** MLB ... I just watch the World Series.
- **Favorite college other than KU:** University of Texas
- **Favorite sport besides football:** As a hobby, I really enjoy playing tennis or golf.
- **Latest book you have read:** "Shantaram" by David Gregory Roberts
- **Favorite NFL player:** Growing up, it was Brett Favre
- **Favorite NBA player:** It's got to be Dirk Nowitzki
- **If I could see one sporting event I would ...** go to the World Cup ... be there for more than a match.
- **If I weren't a football player I would ...** have been a baseball player
- **If I wasn't trying to continue playing football I would ...** be going to graduate school to get my MBA and finding some sort of job I didn't completely hate.

- **Favorite vacation spot:** So far the favorite place I have been is Copenhagen, Denmark.
- **If I could travel anywhere in the world** ... it would be Southeast Pacific, New Zealand, Thailand, Indonesia, Singapore, that whole region.
- **PC or Mac:** I have been a PC, but I think I am switching to Mac.
- **Best barbecue:** Ribs
- **Best barbecue joint:** Little place back at home called Opie's in Spicewood, Texas
- **Favorite place for breakfast in Lawrence:** First Watch
- **Favorite place for lunch in Lawrence:** Quinton's
- **Favorite place for dinner in Lawrence:** Johnny's
- **Favorite bar in Lawrence:** Johnny's
- **Favorite Tex-Mex place:** Maudie's, the original in Tarrytown in Austin
- **Favorite hamburger:** Dempsey's hamburgers in Lawrence are pretty good.
- **Dream car:** I'm not really a big car guy, whatever gets me from A to B. I would rather spend my money on other things.
- **Favorite class:** The ones where I got As in them, more than half. I got one C in high school and one in college. But I deserved the C in college because I did not try at all. It was in the summer and both the midterms were optional and I skipped both of them.

  My final was 100 percent of my grade, and I didn't start looking at the stuff until the night before.
- **Best chicken-fried steak:** The Wheel (in Lawrence)
- **The letters KU or a Jayhawk on the helmet:** I only had the Jayhawk for one game. I think using them both would be cool, switching them out.
- **Favorite KU uniform combination:** The all-white we wore at the Insight.com Bowl and against Missouri. But you need the black spat on the shoe. That is essential, too.

Todd Reesing's Honors

2009

National Football Foundation Scholar Athlete
Honorable mention All Big 12 Conference
Davey O'Brien Semifinalist
Unitas Golden Arm Semifinalist
Manning Award watch list
Maxwell Award watch list
East-West Shrine Game
Academic All Big 12 Conference
Campbell Trophy Finalist

Texas quarterback Colt McCoy and Todd at the National Football Foundation awards dinner following the 2009 season when he was honored as a finalist for the Campbell Trophy for academic achievement.

2008
Davey O'Brien Award semifinalist
Academic All Big 12 Conference
Walter Camp Player of the Year watch list
Maxwell Award watch list
KU Offensive Player of the Year

2007
Davey O'Brien Award Semifinalist
Second team all Big 12 Conference
Academic All Big 12 Conference
KU Offensive MVP

2009 National rankings
No. 4 in Total Offense with 311.25 yards per game
No. 6 in Passing Yardage with 301.33 per game

2008 National Rankings
No. 7 in Passing Yardage with 299.08 per game
No. 8 in Total Offense with 316.31 yards per game
No. 9 in Pass Completions with 25.31 per game

Western Michigan quarterback Tim Hiller, NFL Hall of Famer Archie Manning, Texas quarterback Colt McCoy, and Florida quarterback Tim Tebow (L-R) were with me at the National Football Foundation Awards dinner.

Todd Reesing Career Statistics

PASSING

Year	G	Att	Comp	Int	Pct.	Yds	TD	LG
2006	3	24	14	3	.583	204	3	42
2007	13	446	276	7	.619	3486	33	82
2008	13	495	329	13	.665	3888	32	69
2009	12	496	313	10	.631	3,616	22	74
Totals	41	1,461	932	33	.638	11,194	90	82

RUSHING

Year	Attempts	Yards	Average	Touchdowns	Longest (*yards*)
2006	13	106	8.2	2	63
2007	92	197	2.1	3	53
2008	126	224	1.8	4	18
2009	104	119	1.1	6	22
Totals	335	646	1.9	6	63

TOTAL OFFENSE

Year	Plays	Yds
2006	37	310
2007	538	3,683
2008	621	4,112
2009	600	3,735
Totals	1,796	11,840

I'm so proud to have set so many KU records.

GAME-BY-GAME STATISTICS

	RUSHING				PASSING							
	Att.	Yds.	Avg.	TD	Att	Comp	Pct.	Yds.	Td	Int	Yds/A	Rating
2006 (Record 6-6)												
Northwestern St. W, 49-18	DNP											
La.-Monroe W, 21-19	DNP											
at Toledo L, 37-31	DNP											
South Florida W, 13-7	DNP											
at Nebraska L, 39-32	DNP											
Texas A&M L, 21-18	DNP											
Okla. State L, 42-33	DNP											
at Baylor L, 36-35	DNP											
Colorado W, 20-15	7	90	12.9	1	11	7	63.6	106	2	1	9.6	186.4
at Iowa State W, 41-10	4	14	3.5	1	5	3	60.0	35	1	1	7.0	
Kansas State W, 39-20	DNP											
at Missouri L, 42-17	2	2	1.0	0	8	4	50.0	63	0	1	7.9	
2007 (Record 12-1)												
Central Michigan W, 52-7	6	8	1.3	0	29	20	69.0	261	4	0	9.0	190.1
SE Lousiana W, 62-0	5	31	6.2	0	23	13	56.5	257	2	0	11.2	179.1
Toledo W, 45-13	11	19	1.7	0	35	16	45.7	313	4	0	8.9	158.5
Florida Int'l W, 55-3	8	47	5.9	1	37	23	63.2	368	1	1	9.7	147.9
at Kansas State W, 30-24	7	16	2.3	0	35	22	62.9	267	3	3	7.6	138.1
Baylor W, 58-10	10	14	1.4	0	31	14	45.2	186	2	0	6.0	116.9
at Colorado W, 19-14	7	84	12.0	0	29	20	69.0	153	1	0	5.3	124.7
at TexasA&M W, 19-11	11	-22	-2.0	0	33	21	63.6	180	0	0	5.5	109.5
Nebraska W, 76-39	4	10	2.5	0	41	30	73.2	354	6	0	8.6	194.0
at OKState W, 43-28	2	-6	-3.0	0	40	27	67.5	308	3	0	7.7	159.0
Iowa State W, 45-7	4	5	1.3	0	26	21	80.8	253	4	0	9.7	213.3
Missouri L, 36-28	6	1	0.2	1	49	28	57.1	349	2	2	7.1	122.3

2008 (Record 8-5)

Florida Int'l W, 40-15	9	15	1.7	0	52	37	71.2	256	3	1	4.9	127.7
Louisiana Tech W, 29-0	4	3	0.8	0	38	32	84.2	412	3	0	10.8	201.3
at South Florida L, 37-34	9	13	1.4	1	51	34	66.7	373	3	1	7.3	144.9
Sam Houston St. W, 38-14	12	17	1.4	1	38	23	60.5	356	2	0	9.4	156.6
at Iowa State W, 35-33	11	20	1.8	0	26	18	69.2	319	3	1	12.3	202.7
Colorado W, 30-14	8	33	4.1	0	34	27	79.4	256	1	0	7.5	152.4
at Oklahoma L, 45-31	13	9	0.7	0	41	24	58.5	342	2	2	8.3	134.9
Texas Tech L, 63-21	6	11	1.8	0	26	16	61.5	154	2	3	5.9	113.6
Kansas State W, 52-21	9	47	5.2	1	23	14	60.9	162	1	1	7.0	125.7
at Nebraska L, 45-35	16	35	2.2	1	30	15	50.0	304	3	1	10.1	161.5
Texas L, 35-7	6	-34	-5.7	0	50	25	50.0	258	1	0	5.2	99.9
at Missouri W, 40-37	11	17	1.5	0	51	37	72.5	375	4	2	7.4	152.4
at Minnesota W, 42-21	12	38	3.2	0	35	27	77.1	313	4	1	8.9	184.3

2009 (Record)

Northern Colo. W, 49-3	13	79	6.1	2	20	13	65.0	208	2	0	10.4	185.4
at Texas-El Paso W, 34-7	3	-15	-5.0	0	41	25	61.0	260	1	1	6.3	117.4
Duke W, 44-16	8	51	6.4	0	41	28	68.3	338	3	0	8.2	161.7
Southern Miss. W, 35-2	13	-26	-2.0	0	41	30	73.2	331	3	1	8.1	160.3
Iowa State W, 41-36	5	12	2.4	1	49	37	75.5	442	4	1	9.0	174.1
at Colorado L, 34-30	7	-48	-6.8	0	51	30	58.8	401	2	1	7.9	133.9
Oklahoma L, 35-13	8	17	2.1	1	42	22	52.4	224	0	3	5.3	82.9
at Texas Tech L, 42-21	13	-11	-0.8	0	35	20	57.1	181	1	0	5.2	110.0
at Kansas State L, 17-10	8	25	3.1	0	41	27	65.9	241	1	1	5.9	118.4
Nebraska L, 31-17	9	42	4.7	1	41	19	46.3	236	1	0	5.8	102.7
at Texas L, 51-20	9	-23	-2.6	0	39	25	64.1	256	0	1	6.6	114.1
Missouri L, 41-39	8	8	1.0	1	55	37	67.3	498	4	1	9.1	163.7

University of Kansas School Records

Career records

Attempts	1,461
Completions	932
Yardage	11,194
Touchdown passes	90
Completion percentage	63.8
Passing yardage per game	273.0

Season Records

Attempts	496 (2009)
Completions	329 (2008)
Yardage	3,888 (2008)
Touchdown passes	33 (2007)
Passing yardage per game	301.3 (2009)

Single-game records

Attempts (No. 2)	55 vs. Missouri 2009
Completions	37 (four times)
Yardage	498 vs. Missouri, 2009
Touchdown passes	6 vs. Nebraska, 2008

TOTAL OFFENSE

TOTAL OFFENSE	Career	Season	Game
Play	1,796	621 (08)	62 (Ranks No. 3)
Yardage	11,840	4,112 (08)	506 vs. Missouri 2009 (No. 2)
Avg. Game	288.8	316.3 (08)	

Miscellaneous records

400-yard passing games	4
300-yard passing games	18
Consecutive games with TD	24
Attempts without interception	213 (2007)

NFL quarterbacks

Fourteen quarterbacks were drafted in the NFL in the spring of 2010. All were taller than Todd Reesing. Only two had passed for more yards or more touchdowns than Reesing in his college career. Armanti Edwards of Appalachian State, the only quarterback less than 6' tall, was drafted for his potential as a wide receiver.

The prototype NFL quarterback stands 6' 3" or taller. In the spring of 2010, of the 122 quarterbacks listed on an NFL roster, only one stood less than 6' tall, Seneca Wallace of the Cleveland Browns. Super Bowl MVP Drew Brees is one of five other quarterbacks who stand 6' tall.

NFL quarterback draft

Round	No.	Player	College	Height	Passing	Pct.	TD	INT
1	1	**Sam Bradford**	Oklahoma	6'4"	NR	NR	2	0
		31 games, 604 of 893 for 8,403 yds.			271.06	67.63	88	16
1	25	**Tim Tebow**	Florida	6'3"	206.79 (50)	67.83	21	5
		55 games, 661 of 995 for 9,285 yards			168.82	66.43	88	16
2	48	**Jimmy Clausen**	Notre Dame	6'3"	310.17 (5)	68	28	4
		35 games, 695 of 1,110 for 8,148 yards		323.8	62.61	60	27	
3	85	**Colt McCoy**	Texas	6'1"	251.5 (25)	70.14	27	12
		53 games, 1,157 of 1,645 for 13,253 yards			250.06	70.33	112	45
3	89	**Armanti Edwards***	Appalachian St.	5'11"	274.25(10*)	67.99	12	7
		51 games, 768 of 1,180 for 10,392 yards			203.76	65.08	74	33
5	155	**John Skelton***	Fordham	6'5"	337.09 (1*)	68.02	40	21
		43 games, 802 of 1,363 for 9,923 yards			230.76	58.84	69	36
5	168	**Jonathan Crompton**	Tennessee		215.38 (40)	58.33	27	13
		35 games, 348 of 629 for 4,187 yards			119.63	55.33	36	22
6	176	**Rusty Smith****	Florida Atlantic	6'5"	259.28 (NR)	57.3	14	5
		45 games, 768 of 1,361 for 10,112 yards			334.71	56.43	76	36
6	181	**Dan LeFevour**	Central Mich.	6'4"	245.57 (26)	69.74	28	7
		53 games, 1,171 of 1,763 for 12,905			243.49	66.42	102	36
6	199	**Joe Webb**	Ala-Birmingham	6'3"	191.58 (65)	59.78	21	8
		37 games, 468 of 792 for 5,771 yards			155.92	59.09	37	25

Round	No.	Player	College	Height	Passing	Pct.	TD	INT
6	204	**Tony Pike**	Cincinnati	6'6"	252.00 (23)	62.42	29	6
		27 games, 421 of 682 for 5,018 yards			185.85	61.73	49	20
6	209	**Levi Brown**	Troy	6'3"	327.23 (2)	63.69	23	9
		23 games, 522 of 861 for 5,970 yards			273.22	62.89	38	12
7	239	**Sean Canfield**	Oregon St.	6'4"	251.62 (24)	67.94	21	7
		36 games, 552 of 861 for 5,970 yards			165.83	64.11	38	26
7	250	**Zac Robinson**	Okla. St.	6'2"	173.67 (77)	59.8	15	12
		45 games, 610 of 999 for 8,317 yards			184.82	61.06	66	31
		Todd Reesing	Kansas	5'10"	301.33 (6)	63.1	22	10
		41 games, 932 of 1,461 for 11,194 yards			273.02	63.8	90	32

* Former Division IA
** Injured final six games

Small quarterbacks in the NFL following the 2010 NFL draft

5'-11"
Seneca Wallace, Cleveland
6'-0"
Drew Breese. New Orleans
Chase Daniel, New Orleans
D.J. Shockley, Atlanta
Troy Smith, Baltimore
Michael Vick, Philadelphia
Pat White, Miami

About
the
Authors

AUTHORS

Todd Reesing

*T*odd passed for more yards and touchdowns than any quarterback in Kansas Jayhawks history. More importantly, he was the quarterback on the first Jayhawk team ever to be ranked as high as No. 2 in the Associated Press college football poll. He quarterbacked the Jayhawks to back-to-back bowl games for the first time in school history, leading the Jayhawks to wins in the Orange Bowl against Virginia

Tech following the 2007 season and in the Insight.com Bowl against Minnesota following the 2008 season. He graduated from KU with a double major in economics and finance. Todd grew up in Austin, Texas, where he was the Texas 4A Player of the Year as a junior at Lake Travis High School in Austin.

Kent Pulliam

*K*ent spent more than 30 years as a sports journalist for *The Kansas City Star.* He has won several writing awards from the Associated Press Sports Editors and the Missouri Press Association. He lives in Westwood Hills, Kansas, with his wife, Gina. This is his second book.